Contents

First published in 1997
Second edition 1998
Third edition 1999

Reprinted 2000

Kogan Page Limited
120 Pentonville Road
London
N1 9JN

The Institute of Directors accepts no responsibility for the opinions expressed by the author of this publication. Readers should consult their advisers before acting on any of the issues raised.

British Library Cataloguing in Publication Data

A CIP record for this book is available from the British Library.

ISBN 0 7494 3109 1

Typeset by Jean Cussons Typesetting, Diss, Norfolk
Printed and bound by Clays Ltd, St Ives plc

Preface

The Internet is critical to the business community. It is the focal point of the information revolution that is sweeping through the world and, even in its infancy, is fundamentally reshaping the way we live and do business.

Less than a decade ago, the Internet was primarily viewed as an entertainment vehicle, and someone in business was less likely to know their way around cyberspace than their school-age children. With the arrival of the 21st century, however, this is all changing. The Internet has matured into the fastest growing marketplace in the world and it won't be long before it becomes the main mechanism for commercial transactions; both with consumers and between businesses. To reinforce this, it is predicted that, by the year 2002, e-business (business over the Internet) will generate more than US$1.1 trillion in revenue.

While the Internet's potential is revealing itself so too is the necessity for the business world to re-evaluate how it operates. To retain the competitive edge into the next millennium, it is crucial for businesses to understand that the Internet is more about the way we do business than the actual technology itself. To thrive, or perhaps even to survive, we must all get to grips with the rapidly developing new business environment that the Internet has instigated. Rather than be daunted, though, the business community should view changes brought about by the Internet as an opportunity, and one that should be seized to improve competitiveness and, ultimately, profits.

The year 2000 will see an estimated 200 million people across the world connected to the Internet. Faced with a statistic like this, it is hardly surprising that large companies have already caught on to the potential of the Internet and are investing heavily in creating Web presences. One in three of the world's top 200 consumer brands is already active in cyberspace and it is estimated that more than 70 per cent of large companies will be carrying out sales over the Net by 2002. One of the most significant benefits of the Internet though is that it empowers small businesses – even sole traders – to compete on an even keel with much larger businesses. In the electronic marketplace, where the potential is there to link anyone to anyone, regardless of who or where they are in the world, the rules of competition are different.

The Internet is:

● opening up a truly global marketplace;

● giving businesses the ability to attract and do business with new customers and clients from sources outside traditional markets;

● introducing a level of flexibility that is unparalleled in traditional working environments;

● revolutionizing the pace at which we do business.

Quite simply, a firm with an Internet presence is open for business 24 hours a day, 365 days a year, and in almost every destination from Shanghai to Solihull.

The scope of the Internet

When we talk about doing business on the Internet, most of us immediately associate this with putting together a Web site. But this is just one strand of doing business on the Internet, and one that is clearly not going to be relevant to all small businesses. The Internet is more about improving and increasing the capacity for interaction; putting people and companies in touch with another so they can share information and do business, and at a much faster rate.

The Internet:

● acts as a powerful research tool, giving instant access to news, business and academic information, market intelligence and so on from all over the world;

● enables an individual or a business to send or receive e-mails, including attached documents, images and music in digital form, to or from almost anywhere in the world. This revolutionizes delivery times and dramatically cuts costs;

● gives businesses the opportunity to buy and sell goods and services all over the globe. The Internet can be used to source new markets and find out about products, and also for carrying out e-commerce: where digital goods and services are traded and paid for electronically.

UK businesses and the Internet

The Government has made it quite clear that, during the next century, the UK must become a leading nation on the Internet. By 2002, it has set the target of tripling the number of UK small businesses using the Internet to 1 million, and is pledging its commitment to ensure that the online environment is as safe and secure as traditional offline environments are.

At NatWest we are seizing the opportunities presented by emerging technologies and are striving to be at the forefront of developments in the Internet and e-commerce. As the Internet redefines the parameters of the business world, we will deliver cutting edge solutions that will ease the business community's passage into the Information Age.

We are living through an extremely exciting phase of world history. Society is reshaping around us and the pace of change is gaining momentum every day. The impact that the Internet will have on the way we do business cannot be underestimated, and it is because of this that NatWest is sponsoring this edition of *Doing Business on the Internet*.

Peter Ibbetson
Head of NatWest Small Business Services

Note: Statistics are from the DTI and Deloitte Touche Tohmatsu.

Introduction

The Internet provides the most exciting new business opportunity for decades. Using the Internet, you can communicate with any of the 35 million+ users who connect to the Internet across the world. This book will introduce you to this new technology and how to use it, and, importantly, show you the opportunities that are available to a knowledgeable business and how to make the most of them.

Many books claim you can make your millions on the Internet. You cannot – at least, not yet! This book won't tell you a secret route to riches, but it will tell you how to get connected and provide a new marketing channel and sales opportunity.

There are thousands of new companies joining the Internet every week and finding it a rewarding environment. You can use the Internet for the full cycle from coming up with a new product idea to selling the finished product. For example, here are just a few things that you can do easier and faster using the Internet:

- carrying out research before you launch a new marketing campaign;

- checking patents, demographics or statistics on a new sales area;

- researching new manufacturers and distributors;

- creating a new way of marketing your products to a niche group of users;

- publicizing your company and its products;

- keeping in touch with your customers and employees;

- keeping in touch with the office when you travel;

- cutting long-distance phone bills.

This book covers all these points and more. You can see how to register your company name on the Internet, how to create an online marketing strategy, whether you should set up your own in-house server or use an external company, and how to create an effective

World Wide Web (WWW) site. I'll show you the basics of how to design and write Web pages – including neat tips on good design and using images.

Security is one of the big worries for any new business that links to the Internet. I've covered the risks and how to minimize them and shown you how to use technologies such as firewalls that prevent hackers getting into your company network.

Of course, to use the Internet you need to get connected! I've covered this area in detail, and explained how to choose, configure and use the different types of software you need to browse the WWW or send electronic mail.

The Internet is an exciting new prospect that your business cannot ignore. Whether you choose to use it as a research tool, a marketing tool or as a new sales system it will help change the way you work. This book will explain the ways you can use the power of the Internet and make the most of the technology without breaking any etiquette rules that would get you 'flamed' with a mass of rude messages!

I find the Internet fascinating and work with it to help companies set up on the Internet. It was enjoyable and instructive to write this book – I hope you find it just as interesting to read.

Introduction to the third edition

Welcome to the third edition of *Doing Business on the Internet*. Since the publication of the last edition, business users of the Internet will have seen many changes. Perhaps the most obvious – and certainly the most important for small business – is the growth of e-commerce and online shopping. Customers are now happy to order and pay for goods via a Web site, especially if there's an incentive – such as a discount for Web orders – and are confident of the security measures. One of the reasons behind this growth is the availability of new systems that allow companies to set up an Internet shop easily and cheaply. You can spend a lot of money creating the perfect custom shop, but now you can also test the market for minimal outlay – some suppliers will even set you up for free!

As the Internet matures and grows, it is now, more than ever, essential that every business has an Internet policy. I hope that this book will give you ideas, answers and inspiration to start doing business on the Internet.   **Simon Collin**
simon@pcp.co.uk

The Future of the Internet

The Internet has been developing at a fantastic pace over the past 10–15 years. Since the technology changes so fast, it's difficult to predict where it will go. In this small section I hope to give you a very brief overview of where the technology is likely to lead and how you can keep up!

At the moment, you need a computer to connect to the Internet. In the first edition, I talked about the arrival of network computers (NCs), which were widely hailed as the new way of accessing the Internet. These have not taken off as predicted. Instead, the next development is from television manufacturers who are providing new TV sets that can use the Internet and allow a viewer to browse the Web or send electronic mail messages. We are also now starting to see compact desk telephones that include a fold-out mini-keyboard and screen. These allow users to send and receive e-mail messages without having to use a standard computer.

For ultimate portability, several companies are working on ways to include electronic mail displays on public phone kiosks that will let anyone connect to their mailbox and read or send messages across the Internet. In a similar move, many communications companies have been working on a network of satellites in orbit around the world that will allow you to carry a personal digital assistant (PDA) in your pocket and receive e-mail messages anywhere in the world.

Lastly, the Internet is beginning to change to suit business requirements. To start with, it was unregulated and unruly. Now, slowly, the larger software companies are bringing business features and security to the Internet so that businesses can work securely on the Internet and trust it as a business tool.

The Internet – a Primer

The Internet could prove to be a great resource for your company – if you know how to access it and use it efficiently. In this chapter, you will see how the Internet works, what it can be used for and how to connect to it. This chapter also gives a good idea of the features that the Internet can deliver to your business – in research, marketing, advertising and sales.

Read through this chapter for a concise primer to see how the Internet works and how you can get connected.

What is the Internet?

The Internet is often described in terms of complex communications channels, but it's easier to think of it as you would the telephone system. The Internet is not a single computer; instead it's the net result of tens of thousands of computers linked together. The Internet is often drawn as a symbol that looks rather like a cloud – and this gives you an idea that it's not precisely defined. If a new computer is added to the Internet, the 'cloud' grows.

Each of these tens of thousands of computers are called servers (domain name servers (DNS), to be precise). Each server is assigned a unique address that's made up of a series of numbers. What makes the Internet so useful is that each server automatically maintains an address book that contains the addresses of every other server linked to the Internet. This vast address book is updated automatically to keep every server in touch with new computers that are linked and assigned a new address.

If you want to get on to the Internet, you are really asking to connect to one of the servers that forms part of the Internet. Once you are connected to one server, you can use special commands to explore any other server linked to the Internet. Best of all, because your local server has an address book of all the other servers, you can send electronic mail messages to anyone else on the Internet, not just on your server.

This rather dry introduction to the Internet is essential, but has probably thrown up as many questions as it has answered. Before we go any further, I will try and answer some of the major points of confusion about the way the Internet works.

How the Internet works

When you connect to the Internet, you actually connect to a server. This server is normally owned by a communications company – such as CompuServe, AOL, or Demon. These companies are called Internet Service Providers (ISPs) and they are the middle-men between the Internet and the end-user. If you want to connect directly to the Internet, you can – but you'll need money and resources (as described in Chapter 11).

Each individual communications company – the Internet Service Provider – has a powerful computer running 24 hours a day (one of

CompuServe provides access to the Internet and its own forums

the servers mentioned earlier) that forms a small part of the Internet. This server has an address book of all the other servers on the Internet and has many jobs – such as to ensuringe that electronic mail is delivered correctly. Because there are thousands of users dialling into the ISP computer, it needs a high-speed link to the other servers on the Internet. This is provided by a communication company that uses a high-speed satellite or fibre-optic cable to link countries. If you want a permanent high-speed communications link between London and New York you have plenty of companies to choose from – not just British Telecom.

Windows 95 includes software to get online

The way your home computer links to the Internet is rather like the way your home telephone links to the world – it is connected to the local telephone company exchange that is connected to the main telephone network.

So far, I have talked about the user's end of the Internet. However, the foundations of the Internet is a small group of companies that provide high-speed links between major points around the globe. These links can transmit data often around 10 or 100 times faster than your office network and can carry thousands of individual phone calls. These links ensure that each country is linked and that data can move around the world. However, the coverage, although widespread, is not very local. This is where your ISP steps in. A company that wants to provide Internet services for the general public will set up a server and connect it to the major carriers mentioned above. If you or your business wants to connect to the Internet you will normally connect to the ISP. Just like electricity or gas, if you are a small customer you connect with the local distributor; if you are a major company that wants to get on the Internet you can probably negotiate a deal with the carrier.

Getting on the Internet

To get on to the Internet, you need to set up an account with one of the ISP companies. This is just like setting up a new phone line: you normally pay a monthly rental to the ISP for the use of their computer services. To actually connect to the ISP you need to equip your computer with a modem which will dial the ISP and allow you to send and receive data over a normal telephone line. (There are ways of getting extra performance by using other communication systems, but the phone is convenient, relatively cheap and your business has already has got one installed.)

You now have almost everything you need to connect to the Internet: an account with the ISP that is paid monthly and a modem to link your computer to the phone network. The last piece of the jigsaw is to install the correct software. You will need software that can control the modem and dial the ISP's computer and so look after the nitty-gritty side of communications. You'll also need software that lets you send and receive electronic mail and software that lets you view information stored on any other server computer on the Internet. The types of software available are covered in Chapter 2.

What is electronic mail?

Electronic mail has got to be one of the most useful benefits of the Internet. You can send messages, files or documents to any other user on the Internet – for a minimal cost. The recipient can be in the next building or across the Atlantic, and the most it will cost is the price of a local phone call. Once you have discovered the benefits of electronic mail, you'll wonder why you are still using a fax machine or the postal system.

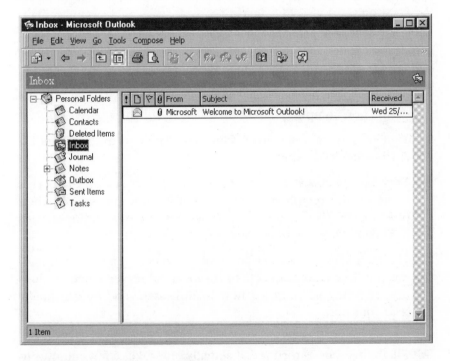

Sophisticated e-mail using Outlook

Before going any further, it's worth clearing up a common misconception about the way electronic mail works. Every user on the Internet has a unique address that identifies their local server (the ISP domain name server described earlier) and also identifies their name on that server. For example, an address might be 'simon@pcp.co.uk'. This identifies the user 'simon' at the domain server called 'pcp'. The last part of the address 'co.uk' identifies the type of server (in this case a company – see the appendix for the full list of suffixes) based in the UK.

If you send an electronic mail message to someone else on the Internet who is in a different country then the process works like this:

1. You use e-mail software on your computer to write a message.

2. You connect to the Internet and send your message to your ISP's main server.

3. The message will be temporarily stored on the ISP's server while it checks its address book to make sure that the delivery address is correct.

4. If the server doesn't find the address, the message is returned to you.

5. If the server does find the address, the server will work out the best (normally the cheapest) route across the world to get to the destination computer.

6. Your message is transferred from one server to the next until it reaches its destination.

7. Now your message has arrived at the correct server; the server looks up the recipient's name and stores the message in their postbox (this is actually just a folder or directory on the server's hard disk where incoming messages are stored).

8. The recipient still doesn't know he has received a new mail message until he next connects to his local ISP server. Once he does this, he'll be told there's a new mail message and he can finally read your note.

Although this sounds tortured, it actually only takes a few minutes to send a message from, say, London to Los Angeles – although it might be days before the recipient bothers to log on to the Internet and discover they have mail. Obviously, it defeats the object if you have to telephone your friend in LA to tell him he has a message, so the only rule to using electronic mail is to check your postbox regularly – every day, if possible.

What's the World Wide Web?

The World Wide Web (often shortened to WWW or W3 or just the 'Web') is the good-looking part of the Internet. As you've discovered, the Internet is really just a collection of computers linked together across the world. The WWW is a way of ensuring that the information stored on all the computers can be accessed by just about anyone.

The WWW looks good and is easy to use

The real surge in the popularity of the Internet is almost entirely due to the WWW. Just a few years ago, before the WWW, the Internet existed in a healthy, growing state, but you could only view information in the form of text – pages and pages of text. If you wanted to move from one page to another, you would have to type in a command and retrieve another page of text. Not very exciting.

The WWW has done for the Internet what Microsoft Windows and the Macintosh did for personal computers – it's given the Internet a graphical front-end that you can navigate with a mouse and that's easy to use and understand. Now, information stored on the computers around the Internet is stored in the form of pages. Each page can contain graphics, text, animations, video and even sound clips. You can access a page if you know its address and click on text or buttons to move to another linked page.

To achieve this, there have been two basic changes to the way information is presented on the Internet. As I mentioned, data is now stored in the form of pages; each page is formatted by the page's designer using a set of codes called HTML (hypertext mark up language). These codes describe, for example, whether text should be in bold type, where to insert a graphic image or how to display a link to another page.

In order to view these pages, you'll need a WWW browser application. This software runs on your computer and decodes the HTML instructions to display the formatted page. Some WWW browsers are available free – Microsoft includes its Internet Explorer software with Windows 95 and Netscape supplies a limited version of its Navigator software; other software will cost you a nominal charge.

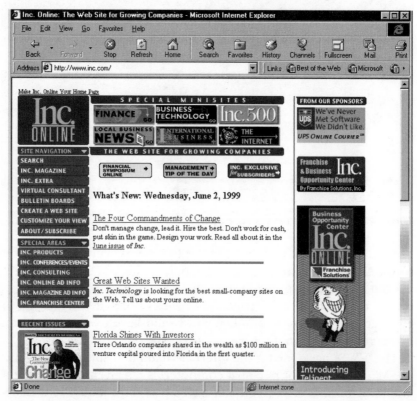

Magazines and business archives on the WWW

To summarize, the World Wide Web is a way of arranging information into individual pages that can be hyper-linked (a button or keyword on one page links to information on another page). The individual pages can have graphics, video or animations embedded together with colour and text formatting – these are defined by the designer using special codes. The user views a WWW page using a browser that will decode these marks to display the finished page.

What is on the Internet?

There is so much information available on the Internet that it can hardly be catalogued! In addition to access to over 35 million users who that have electronic mail accounts, you can look at the information and products of thousands of different companies. There are online databases that cover government statistics, financial information, share prices, patent details, marketing sources, distributors and more. For leisure, there are databases of cinemas, books, fan-clubs, houses for sale and rent, cars for sale and more. Lastly, there are newsgroups that keep you up to date with what your peers in a particular

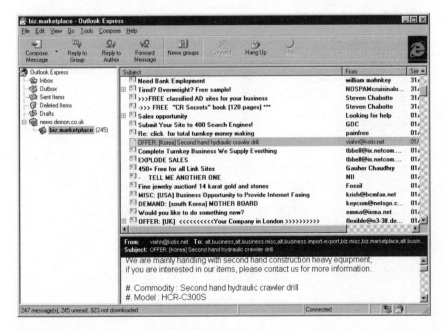

Reading the business newsgroup topics

profession are discussing. These newsgroups are forums for discussion and are one of the most active parts of the Internet.

In short, you can use the Internet to find out the weather anywhere in the world, keep up to date with instant world news, track share prices, research prospective clients, check on credit status, discuss problems with others in your profession, keep up with new developments and, of course, market your own company!

2

Getting Online

Throughout the rest of this book, I have covered the benefits, resources and opportunities of the Internet, but this chapter covers the business of how you actually connect to the Internet and get online.

In this chapter, I will explain how a small company or individual can get on to the Internet. This will let you create your own Web site, browse other sites, send electronic mail and look at the thousands of newsgroups. If, however, you are a larger company or a small company with a lot of data to share on the Internet or you want to provide real-time data (changing or live data) to a complex Web site, then you will probably want your own Internet server. This subject and related topics (such as leased-line links) are covered in Chapter 12.

There are really just two ways to get connected to the Internet – you can set up an account with an Internet Service Provider (ISP) that provides a direct link to the Internet or you can set up an account with an Online Service Provider (OSP) that offers a route to the Internet. Each has benefits and disadvantages. I'll start by defining the two types of company that you might deal with.

Online Service Providers (OSPs)

An OSP runs its own large computer system which includes hundreds of its own databases and resources. A good example is CompuServe; this system runs on several large, powerful computers in the USA and contains databases on hundreds of different subjects. You have to pay extra to search these databases, but they are regularly maintained by reputable companies. For example, there are databases of company credit information maintained by Dunn & Bradstreet.

In addition to the databases, an OSP also has forums that let you discuss a subject with the other users. CompuServe has thousands of forums covering everything from teaching to programming; they are well-supported by software manufacturers who use them as a way of answering problems. OSPs also have file areas where you can download programs and documents. Lastly, OSPs also provide electronic mail facilities to the other users registered with the OSP.

As you can see, an OSP provides a service rather like the Internet itself, but contained in one place and with reliable information (the Internet is not governed, nor is the information it contains guaranteed).

All OSPs have now provided links to the Internet so that their registered users can browse the Internet and send electronic mail to users on the Internet or register with other services. The effect of these links means that if you sign up with a traditional OSP such as AOL or CompuServe you get all its information and full access to the Internet.

There are a few restrictions that will put off many businesses from joining an OSP. Firstly, although you can create your own Web pages, you do not get all the features offered by ISPs – such as counters, access logs and scripts that enhance your Web site. Most importantly, you cannot have your own domain name – although this is likely to change in the next year. This means that you cannot advertise your Web site as 'www.yourname.com'; instead you have to advertise the address to your Web site as 'www.compuserve.com/yourname'. It doesn't sound quite as professional or polished.

There are a few extra drawbacks to an OSP. The first is that they generally do not support high-speed links, such as ISDN or leased line, so are a poor choice for a business that wants to link several users to the Internet. Also, OSPs normally charge by the minute, so the longer you browse the Internet the more you pay. ISPs charge a flat fee per month or year regardless of the time you spend online.

In their favour, especially for users that travel, OSPs are very big companies and have local telephone numbers in just about every country. CompuServe is one of the best, with local numbers all over the world. This means that if you travel, you can always dial into a local number to pick up your new mail messages; without this you would have to dial back to the UK or USA where your ISP is based. Some users (myself included!) have two accounts – an ISP account for the main business and an OSP account used when travelling. (As an alternative to using an OSP for travelling, you could use a global

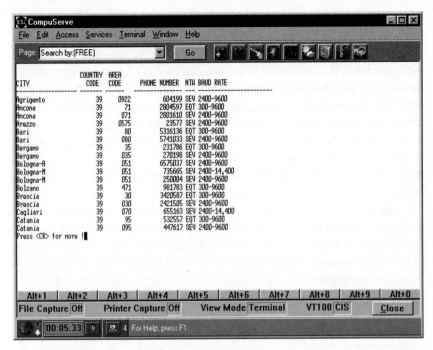

CompuServe has worldwide access numbers

roaming service supported by may ISPs. Companies such as MCI WorldNet (www.worldnet.com) and Ipass (www.ipass.com) provide access numbers in many different countries.)

Changing face of OSPs

Over the past year, Online Service Providers have changed many of their features to provide a better service to users that want to use the Internet. CompuServe has now been bought by AOL (although the two companies are still marketed separately).

A new breed of OSP has arrived that offers all the benefits of both an OSP and an ISP; the major players include MSN (Microsoft Network) and LineOne.These companies offer a standard service that lets you connect to the Internet, send e-mail, browse Web pages – all for a fixed monthly fee. However, you also have access to private databases for news, support and discussion forums.

Internet Service Providers (ISPs)

An ISP offers a very different type of service to an OSP. It has a smaller computer system that links directly on to the Internet via a high-speed link. The ISP computer system does not normally have any files or databases of its own – it really is just a link to the Internet. If you sign up with an ISP such as Demon, Pipex, BT Internet or Global Internet you will receive a list of access telephone numbers to dial into the ISP computer using your computer and a modem. That's often all you get! Some ISPs are friendlier and will send you a starter pack with all the software you need, hopefully pre-configured; others leave you on your own.

When you sign up to have an account with an ISP you will get a user name and a certain amount of disk space on the ISP's computer, on which you can store your Web pages. You will be known to the world as 'yourcompany.demon.co.uk' or something similar; however, you can pay extra (normally around £200 per year) and register your own domain name, which means you will be known to the world as 'yourcompany.com'.

With an ISP account you can send and receive electronic mail to any other Internet user – including users with OSP accounts – and you can browse any Web page on the Internet, download files and look at newsgroups.

The larger ISPs will have support for high-speed links between your business and their system, supporting ISDN and leased lines. These are essential if you want to link your office network to the Internet or to provide your own Web server.

For businesses based in one place, an ISP account is a better bet than an OSP. However, if some of your employees travel extensively, you might find it useful to have an OSP account just to save costly telephone calls back to your country: ISPs are not good at providing worldwide access numbers outside your country.

Lastly, ISPs are normally cheaper than OSPs – especially for heavy users of the Internet. They will generally charge you a fixed monthly fee and that's all. There is no extra charge based on the time you spend on the Internet.

The arrival of free ISPs in the UK and in parts of the United States has begun to shake up the established players. However attractive these free services are for consumers, they are not always suitable for business users. Free ISPs provide full Internet access, with a local telephone number access point, to almost anyone who applies. They rely on advertising and a percentage of the telephone call charge to pay for their services.

The main drawback of free ISPs is that they do not (yet) allow you

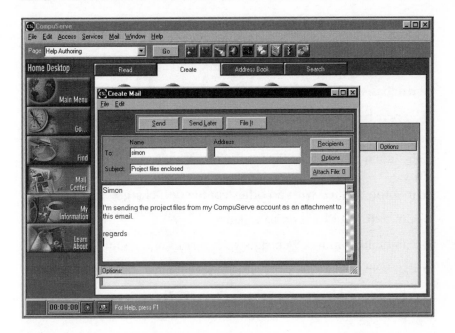

The CompuServe e-mail software

to set up a domain name or complex Web sites (you cannot integrate database access, for example). There are, however, ways in which a free ISP might be useful; for example, if you currently store your Web site using a company that does not provide modem access – companies such as Tabnet, Rapidsite, or Virtual Internet – then you will need a second account with an ISP to dial into the Internet to collect your e-mail or update your Web site. Your Web Site and domain name remain in the same place, but you could switch you dial-up access to any of the free ISPs, saving the monthly subscription.

Pros and cons

OSP – such as CompuServe, AOL
Pros:
● friendly software that is easy to use and set up;

● local access telephone numbers spread around the world;

● own reputable databases and forums.

Cons:
- do not get your own domain name;
- often charged according to the time you are connected;
- databases are normally a chargeable extra;
- expensive for more than occasional use of the Internet.

ISP – such as Demon, Pipex or Global
Pros:
- monthly flat fee with no other connection charges;
- can have your own domain name;
- can build complex Web sites with scripts and counters;
- can help businesses with custom solutions;
- support for high-speed links such as ISDN and leased lines.

Cons:
- normally do not have worldwide access numbers, so long-distance calls required when travelling;
- do not always provide starter software;
- no online resources of their own.

Choice chart

Here are a few examples of users and the type of service that they might prefer:

1. **Business wanting to promote itself on the Internet.** This company should use an ISP account and register its own domain name for its Web site and electronic mail.

2. **Business researcher who needs to send electronic mail messages.** This person might be better off with an OSP that has online business databases and links to the Internet for occasional use of newsgroups.

3. **Business person who travels around one country but needs to keep in touch by sending electronic mail messages and checking his Web site.** This person would be better

off with an ISP account, since they provide good coverage in their country for a fixed monthly fee.

4. **Business traveller who travels abroad regularly and needs to keep in touch with his office.** An OSP would save money, since they normally provide extensive worldwide access telephone numbers, rather than a long-distance call back to the ISP.

5. **Marketing department that needs to check competition and carry out basic research.** For users who spend a lot of time online, it would be cheaper to use an ISP with fixed monthly costs.

6. **Office full of users with occasional Internet use and electronic mail.** An ISP would be able to provide an high-speed link (ISDN or leased line) between the office and its system for full Internet access at a fixed cost.

What you need to get online

To get connected to the Internet, you will need a computer, a modem (or ISDN device), a mouse and – preferably – a colour screen. In reality, most users will have the basic equipment and will need to buy a modem. In addition to this equipment, you will need special software to control the hardware and let you browse the Internet.

Software requirements

1. **TCP/IP or socket manager.** Once configured, you'll never see this mysterious piece of software. It is used to dial the ISP or OSP and establish a connection. It then looks after the process of moving data to and fro. If you have Microsoft Windows 95/98, this software is included free. MS-DOS, Windows 3.x and Macintosh users will need to contact their ISP to get hold of this software. OSPs normally provide this as part of a start-up kit.

2. **Electronic mail software.** This lets you send and receive electronic mail messages and send files as attachments. Windows 95 users have this built in. Other DOS, Windows and Macintosh users can get free or shareware software to do the same job from CD ROMS on computer magazines or by downloading software from the Internet (see appendix of resources).

3. **WWW browser.** This lets you view any Web page on the Internet. Most browsers including Microsoft IE and Netscape Communicator include a full-featured e-mail program. Windows 95/98 includes the Microsoft Internet Explorer free. Netscape Navigator now supplies both its basic and more feature-rich versions free of charge. Other browsers can be bought from computer shops or, sometimes, are available for download for a trial period.

4. **News reader.** This lets you view the 40,000-odd newsgroups and read or post a message. Microsoft supplies its news reader software free with its IE Web browser and Netscape bundles a news reader with its Communicator browser. Alternative products are generally available free to download (search the 'www.download.com' site).

5. **FTP.** This utility lets you transfer files over the Internet. You can use it to transfer files from a remote computer to your desktop (download) or to send Web pages you have created on your desktop to the ISP (upload). Most WWW browsers can handle simple downloads using FTP, but to upload files to your Web site you'll need a special utility that you can download or get free (search the 'www.download.com' site).

6. **Telnet.** This lets you connect to your ISP's computer and enter commands as if you were sitting at their computer. It's used when setting up your Web site – for example, to make a directory or change the security attributes of Web files. You will need a special program to use Telnet – Windows 95 includes its own version (select Start/Run/Telnet) and many other versions are available as shareware.

7. **Plug-ins.** These are small programs that work with your Web browser to add new functionality, for example allowing it to play multimedia files such as sound or video clips. These are available from various sites – when you need one, you'll see a message appear and you will normally be given the option to download the plug-in.

When choosing your service provider, you should look not only at the type of service they provide, but also the software they will provide. For example, CompuServe supplies everything you need to use its system and the Internet. Other service providers sometimes provide some of the software or charge for software. If you are looking to use a service provider for your business, then free software is not as important as the speed of connections, price of the service and type of service offered. However, if you want a single account to try out the Internet, you will find it far simpler to sign up with a provider that offers a complete package.

Choosing your computer

Using the Internet does not require a particularly powerful computer – you are only looking at text sent from a distant computer. For a PC you really need to be able to run Microsoft Windows since most Internet software is designed to run under Windows. If you are stuck with DOS you can send electronic mail and read newsgroups, but you won't be able to view the colourful graphics that make the WWW interesting.

You can access the Internet from any type of computer: a desktop, laptop or even a hand-held PDA (personal digital assistant) such as a Psion or Palm computer.

If you are planning to buy a new PC, it should be supplied with Windows 98 pre-installed. There are two brands of main processor available from Intel and AMD. The processor does the hard work inside the PC. The power of your PC is partly determined by the clock speed of the processor, measures in MHz. Currently, the fastest processor is a Pentium III running at 500MHz or more. However, for most business applications, a slightly slower Pentium II or AMD K-6 based PC running at 250–400MHz will be more than adequate and will be considerably cheaper.

If you are planning to use existing computers to access the Internet, there are few problems, but make sure that you have the minimum PC requirements.

Minimum PC requirements: ideally your PC should have 8Mb of RAM and a 200Mb hard disk. The main processor should be an 80486 or Pentium, although you can run Windows with a slower 80386. Try and get a colour monitor, an S-VGA graphics adapter (that can display a resolution of at least 800 × 600). Web pages are now designed on the assumption that the user will be viewing it on a screen with a resolution of 800 × 600.

Almost any Macintosh that can run its System 7 or 8 operating system can be connected to the Internet. You can connect older Macs that run System 6, but you will need to buy Apple's TCP/IP software (or a similar program from a third party). For either operating system, you will also need to get hold of electronic mail software, WWW browser, newsgroup reader and FTP software.

Choosing your modem

The one bottleneck that will greatly influence the speed at which you can browse the Internet and transfer data is the modem. A modem converts data from a computer into sound signals that can then be transmitted over a normal telephone line; it works the opposite way around when receiving information.

There are dozens of acronyms that are used by modem manufacturers to tell you the speed at which the modem can transfer information over a telephone line and any other features it might have. Normally, modems also have the ability to send or receive facsimile messages to and from a normal fax machine. Most modems also include error detection and correction features that spot if the data being received has been corrupted (typically by noise and crackles on the telephone line).

If you want to send electronic mail and read newsgroups, you can get by with an older, cheaper, slower modem. However, if you want to look at Web pages which contain lots of graphic images then you will need the fastest modem you can afford to download the data that makes up the images. (It's worth noting that sometimes, even a fast modem will not speed up the data transfer, since the number of other users on the Internet has slowed down the server computers and clogged up the main high-speed links.)

Modem standards

The maximum speed at which a modem can transfer data conforms to one of several possible standard rates. These are given 'V' numbers that are set by an international standards body, CCITT. In addition to the speed at which the modem can operate, there are 'V' numbers that tell you if a modem can compress data (which increases the quantity of data it can transfer) and if it can correct errors. The important codes to look out for when buying a modem are:

- V32: 9,600 bits per second. An older standard that is not fast enough for today's Internet sites.

- V32bis: 14,400 bits per second. You could use this speed most of the time, but you might find it too slow if you manage a Web site or if you look at Web sites with lots of graphic images – they have more data which is slower to download at this speed.

- V34: 28,800 bits per second. This is the current standard for high-speed modems.

- V42: a standard that tells you that the modem can spot errors in the data.

- V42bis: a standard that tells you that the modem can compress data.

- V90: a new data transmission standard that supports high-speed data transfer at up to 56,000 bits per second; similar to the K56 standard.

- X2: a new standard developed by US Robotics for its range of high-speed modems. It can transfer data at 56,000 bits per second.

- K56flex: a new standard developed by Hayes, Pace and other manufacturers for a range of high-speed modems. It can transfer data at 56,000 bits per second; similar to X2.

Fax modems allow you to send a document to another fax machine or to receive a fax sent by a fax machine. A received fax is stored on your computer as a graphic image that you can then read or print out. Most current modems support the fax standards.

ISDN

If you expect heavy use of the Internet, or if you want to connect several users to the Internet, you should look at replacing your modem and using an ISDN adapter. ISDN (Integrated Services Digital Network) is a service offered by your local telephone company and provides a high-speed digital equivalent to a normal telephone line. The advantage of ISDN is that it is between two and four times as fast as the fastest modem, but does not cost as much as a leased line.

To use ISDN you will need to have a special ISDN line installed in your office. This normally costs around £100–£200. Once this has been installed, you can connect your ISDN adapter – around 30 per cent more expensive than a good modem – and connect to the Internet.

Before you install ISDN, make sure that your ISP supports an ISDN link! Many OSPs do not, but the majority of the bigger ISPs will let you link via ISDN – although they will probably charge you more for the privilege.

A call made over an ISDN link is charged at roughly the same rate as a normal telephone call by your telephone operator. The beauty of ISDN is that there is no delay in connecting to the ISP. From the moment you press the Connect button, it takes just a couple of seconds to be online. A normal modem can take over 30 seconds to dial and connect.

Home Highway

In the UK, there is a new step between a standard telephone link and an ISDN line. This new service is called Home Highway and is supplied by BT (www.bt.co.uk). The service converts an existing telephone line into two separate digital lines that can then be used in a similar way to an ISDN line. The advantage is that you get near-instant connection and transfer speeds of up to 64 Kbps. However, there is an initial installation charge and rental for the new equipment. As the name suggests, it is really aimed at enthusiasts or homeworkers who still want to use their existing phone and fax but who also want high-speed surving. For office installations it is probably still better to choose an ISDN link (that can support transfer speeds of up to 128Kbps) for small or medium-sized networks.

Digital lines

One of the most promising new technologies that could revolutionize the way we connect to the Internet is called ADSL. British Telecom and some cable TV suppliers are experimenting with this standard and running trials in some areas. In parts of the United States and in some other countries, ADSL is already available. If you have a local telephone provider that supports ADSL, you should consider this as an alternative to upgrading from ISDN to leased line.

Leased line

The next step up from an ISDN connection is to install a leased line between you and the ISP. Again, you have to check that your ISP supports this service – few do. For the basic service of leased line, there is no speed advantage over an ISDN link – both run at a speed of 64,000 bits per second. The real advantage of a leased line is that it provides a permanent link between you and your ISP that is 'connected' 24 hours per day.

There are no telephone charges with a leased line; instead, you pay a quarterly rental that is around £7,000 per year if you are close to a major city or more if you are further out. For this price, you can stay online day and night with no fear of running up huge telephone bills.

A leased line is most useful for companies that want to connect their own Internet server to the Internet and so need to provide a 24-hour link. If you have a large number of users or if you want to connect your office network to the Internet, you might find it cheaper to install a leased line than to pay a telephone bill.

When using a leased line, you do not use a modem or an ISDN adapter; instead you need to install a router. This box ensures that the data from your computer is correctly formatted and addressed before it is sent to the Internet. A router costs around £1,000.

The final step I will cover in this book is a high-speed leased line. (There are faster links, but these are out of the scope of this book – and the price range of many!) You can opt to install a 2Mb leased line that transfers 2,000,000 bits of data per second – that's over 30 times faster than a standard leased line or ISDN link. Again, you pay a quarterly rental charge and you will need to install a router to transfer the information to the Internet.

Traffic jams and download times

There are many different factors that affect the time it will take to transfer a file across the Internet to your computer. If you had a direct telephone link to the remote computer, then it would be easy to work out the time it would take and you would know that the time taken would come down if you used a faster modem.

Unfortunately, the Internet has its own delays; if there are a lot of other users also trying to download the same file as you, then this will cause delays. If the file is stored on a slow computer, it will slow down the process and, lastly, if the file is stored on a computer in another country, then you are relying on the speed of the links between your ISP and the other country.

You will find that, on average, a 1Mb file will take around 10–20 minutes to download if you have a fast 33.6Kbps modem (7–15 minutes if you have the newest type of 56Kbps high-speed modem). Sometimes, you will pick a file stored on a high-speed computer at a quiet moment on the Internet and it will fly across.

Best time for browsing

As you use the Internet, you might think that it slows down some-times – you are quite right! As more users connect to the Internet, there is more information being transferred and the links cannot always cope with the amount of information. This is most noticeable in the early afternoon when people in the USA wake up and start to connect. From 2 pm onwards, the Internet slows down considerably and any file download will take much longer. The worst time to use the Internet is in the late afternoon: users in the USA are connected and people in the UK are getting home after work and playing with the Internet. The best time is mid-morning – in the early morning the office computers are connected as users check their mail messages. Don't forget, though, that the mid-morning is also the most expensive time for telephone calls. The cheapest time is over the weekend.

Internet software

I described earlier in this chapter the range of software you will need to use to make the most of the Internet. In this section, I'll show you exactly what each software program does and how to configure and use it. If you have chosen a service provider that provides a starter kit with everything supplied, you should still read this section, since you might want to change or upgrade part of your software as new ver-sions become available. The shopping list of utilities that you will need is as follows:

● TCP/IP or socket manager;

● electronic mail software;

● WWW browser;

● news reader;

● FTP;

● Telnet;

● plug-ins.

TCP/IP or socket manager

This little program manages the link between your computer and the ISP. It is called a protocol and formats your data correctly with your address information before sending it off to the Internet. It's an arcane little utility that you will need to configure. It might sound complex, but it's straightforward – and essential.

If you have Windows 95/98 or a Macintosh with System 8 then you have already got a TCP/IP manager. If you have Windows 3.x you'll need to get hold of something called Trumpet Winsock; if you have a Mac with System 6 you'll need Apple's MacTCP or similar. Your ISP should be able to sell you this software.

Under Windows 95/98, the TCP/IP manager is linked to the Windows Dial Up Networking (DUN) manager software. This means that when you start the Microsoft Web browser, it automatically starts the DUN software that dials your ISP, connects and logs in to the Internet. If this does not happen, you will probably need to install the DUN feature – use the Start/Settings/Install option of Windows 95/98 and insert the original Windows CD ROM.

Now you have your software, you need to configure it. First, you have to enter the local access telephone number of your ISP. You will also need to enter your user name, the domain name of the ISP and your user password. All this information will be provided by your ISP when you sign up. You've now configured the software.

When you want to connect to the Internet, the program will dial the ISP's computer, connect and send your user name. The ISP will ask the program for a password, which it will send. Once all this has happened, it will open a connection and manage it in the background. Any other Internet application can be run and will send its data via the TCP/IP software over the connection to the Internet.

Electronic mail software

Electronic mail software lets you send and receive mail messages with other users on the Internet. There are dozens of different types of mail software available. Some are free, others are shareware and some are full commercial products – they all do roughly the same job in slightly different ways.

Some Web browsers – notably Netscape Communicator and Microsoft IE – have mail functions built in. If you want more functionality you can use a separate program. Two of the most popular mail programs are called Eudora and Pegasus. Both are available as free and commercial versions (the commercial products have more features). Whichever product you choose, you'll need to configure it before it can be used. First, you'll need to enter your user name and

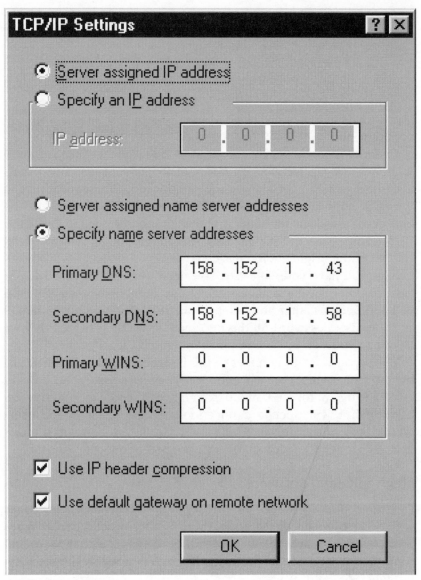

Setting up Windows

password together with the name of the Internet server that will store your electronic mail messages.

For example, if you are user 'simon' and you have a domain name registered with an ISP of 'simon.com' you will need to check the name of the ISP's server that manages mail – for example

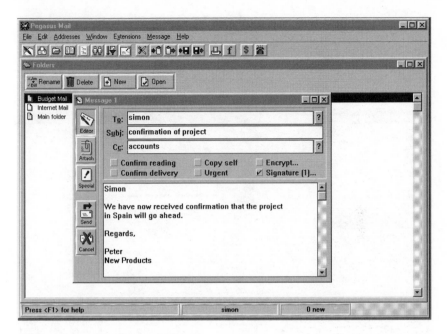

Pegasus e-mail software is free

'post.demon.co.uk' for the Demon computer. You enter all this information into the mail software to allow it to check for new mail and
send messages – both operations are done via the server computer
named. If you have set up your own Internet server in your company, you will have set up a mail program that looks after mail messages; in this case, enter your own server's name.

One warning worth noting. There are several ways of transferring
messages over the Internet, but there are two that are commonly
used to transfer mail messages between an ISP and a user. One is
called SMTP (Simple Mail Transfer Protocol) and the other is called
POP 3. Most ISPs use a combination of the two systems – POP 3 to
send messages and SMTP to receive messages. As a result, most mail
software uses this combination of two standards. But watch out, some
ISPs – such as Demon – use just one standard (SMTP in the case of
Demon). This gives greater flexibility, but means you are very re-
stricted in the choice of mail software that supports SMTP both for
sending and receiving mail.

If you are connecting an office network to the Internet, you might
already have e-mail software installed; if this is the case, you'll need a
gateway between the e-mail post-office program and the Internet.

Programs such as Lotus cc:Mail and Microsoft Mail can have a gateway fitted (at an extra cost). The gateway is a special software program that converts the e-mail to the correct format required for the Internet.

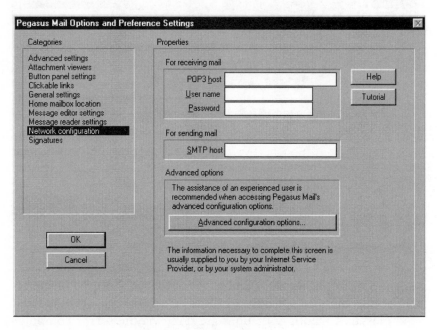

Configuring the way e-mail is transferred

Using electronic mail

To send a mail message to another user, you need their full mail address. This is written in two parts, separated by an '@' symbol. To the left of the '@' symbol is their user name; to the right of the symbol is their company's domain name. For example, you can send me a mail message at the following address 'simon_collin@pcp.co.uk'. The domain name to the right of the '@' symbol is my company's domain name. The company name is PCP, and the letters that follow this tell you what sort of company you are dealing with: '.co' means a company, '.uk' means it's based in the UK. See the appendix for a full list of the types of domain name.

Mail programs normally use folders to organize your mail messages: 'In' for new, incoming mail; 'Sent' for copies of messages you have sent, 'Draft' for messages that you are working on. One feature that's worth setting up, especially if you start receiving a lot of mail

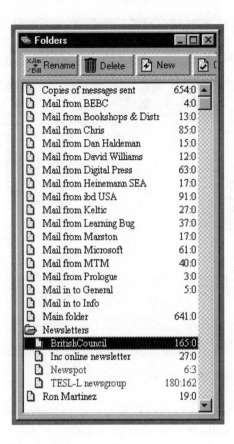

Folders help organize messages

messages, is the filter function that's built into most mail programs.
This will look at each message as it is received and, depending on the
rules you have entered, will save it in a particular folder. This is useful
for organizing messages about a particular project or from a particular person.

WWW browser

A WWW browser (often called a Web browser or just a browser) lets
you view pages on the WWW. What it actually does is to ask a remote
computer to send it a file that contains text and formatting commands which it then interprets and displays as a nicely formatted
result. Browsers can display images, animation and, in some cases,
video and sound. As well as displaying text and pictures, a browser

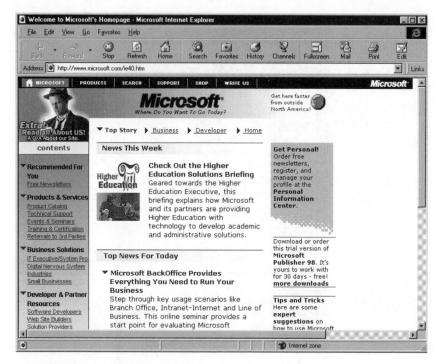

Microsoft's browser and Web site

also lets you click on hotspots that jump to another page (this is called hypertext and is explained in Chapter 10).

All the commands that tell a browser how to format text use a simple language called HTML (hypertext markup language). There are now three versions of HTML – although HTML 2 is still the common standard.

To confuse the issue, the developers of the main browsers decided that the formatting instructions in the HTML language were not enough and so added their own – called extensions. Competing browsers do not always support all of a competitor's extensions. Lastly, some browsers can have extra features included using plug-ins. These, for example, let the browser display video.

Brands of browser

There are several types of browser available, but the two main brands are from Microsoft and Netscape. There are some differences between the two but they will both let you look at Web pages and browse the Web. If you happen to have both types of browser

installed on your computer, you might notice that they sometimes
display the same Web page in a slightly different way, but this does
not normally change the way that you use the page.

Each brand of browser has different versions that support different
levels of HTML codes and different features. For example, Navigator
3 supports some HTML codes, but Navigator 4 supports new, more
complex codes. Both Microsoft and Netscape give away their
browser programs for free.

Windows 95 dialing the ISP

There's very little to configure with your browser. It will automatically detect the TCP/IP manager and communicate with it. If your browser lets you look at newsgroups (Navigator does, IE does not) then you will have to configure the browser with the name of the ISP computer that manages newsgroups.

Using a Web browser

To use a Web browser, you need to enter a URL (Uniform Resource Locator). This often cryptic looking set of codes is the unique address that identifies each Web page on the Internet. For example, the main Web page - called the home page - of Microsoft can be viewed by entering its URL: 'http://www.microsoft.com/'.

Type in a URL to view a page

The first part in this URL is 'http://' - this is actually an instruction to your browser that tells it to use its HTTP commands that are used to access WWW pages (instead of FTP for transferring files). The next part of the code is the unique URL for this site. If you want to access an individual Web page (not the main home page) you will have to enter the file name that contains the Web page. Again, using Microsoft, you might be interested in Excel products and so you would enter 'http://www.microsoft.com/excel.html'. The last two words are the file name for the Web page - they generally end in 'html'.

To confuse the matter further, the first, or home, page of any Web site is always given the file name 'index.html'. Because of this, browsers will look for this file automatically, which is why we did not enter this file name when accessing the Microsoft home page. Entering 'http://www.microsoft.com' is the same as 'http://www.

microsoft.com/index.html'. Another tip is that most browsers auto-matically work out if you are viewing a Web page, so you do not have to enter the 'http://' part – just 'www.microsoft.com'.

News reader

A news reader program lets you view messages posted to any of the 40,000 individual newsgroups. Some WWW browsers – notably Netscape Navigator – have a news reader function built in; if you are using another browser, such as Microsoft's IE, then you'll need to install and configure a separate news reader. Microsoft supplies its Internet News product free of charge – and it's very good.

To configure a news reader (including those built into browsers) you need to enter the name of the ISP server that manages all the news group activity. Each ISP will have a computer that looks after this function and they should tell you its name when you sign up. It's normally called 'news.' followed by the name of the ISP. For example, Demon's server that manages news groups is called 'news.demon.co.uk'. Similarly, CompuServe's server is called 'news.compuserve.com'. The only other information you need to enter is your electronic mail address; this is added to any message you post to a newsgroup.

FTP

FTP (file transfer protocol) is a way of transferring files between two computers linked via the Internet. It's normally used to download a file from a distant computer or to upload your Web pages to your ISP's Internet server.

There are several FTP programs available, all with similar features. Some Web browsers – such as Netscape Navigator – include an FTP function but this can only be used to download files; it cannot nor-mally be used to upload files.

You do not need to configure an FTP program; all you need to enter is the address (the URL) of the computer you want to transfer files from. For example, if you want to download the latest version of Microsoft's Internet Explorer, you would enter 'ftp.microsoft.com' as the destination address. You'll need to enter a user name and pass-word but most computers allow anonymous logins (see Chapter 7). For an anonymous login you enter the user name 'anonymous' and your e-mail address as the password (this works with Microsoft). You will then see a list of files available to download.

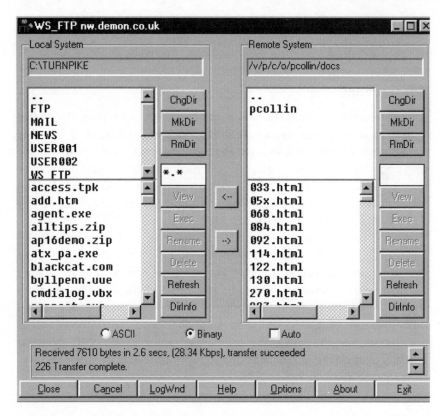

Transferring files using FTP software

If you want to upload files to your Web site, you will need to enter the address of your ISP's computer – this is not the same as your domain name. For example, if your have the domain name of 'www.simon.com' and use Demon as your ISP, you would have to enter the address 'www.demon.co.uk' and then enter your user name 'simon' and the password.

Telnet

Telnet is an unusual program – it lets you control a remote computer and enter commands as if you were sitting at the keyboard in front of that remote computer. For example, if you have an Internet server in London and you have travelled to Boston, you can use Telnet to access your Internet server and enter standard Unix commands to list files, delete or copy files, and run programs.

There are many Telnet programs available – normally as freeware

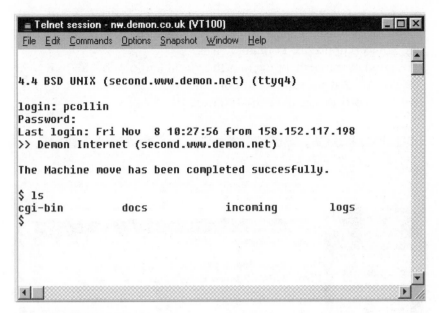

Telnet provides remote access

or shareware. Like an FTP program, there is nothing to configure. You have to enter the destination address of the computer that you want to access, together with your user name and password.

Plug-ins

Plug-ins are tiny programs that add extra functionality to your browser (see earlier in this chapter). Plug-ins are normally downloaded and installed automatically. A plug-in extends the features supported by a Web browser. For example, it might allow you to view live moving video clips, listen to live audio or playback a multimedia animated sequence.

If you visit a Web site that has decided to make use of exciting new multimedia features, you will probably need a plug-in. The Web site should be able to automatically detect if you have the correct plug-in installed. If you do not, it should tell you that you will need to download the plug-in and ask if you want to continue. Since this is a potential security risk (downloading an unknown application on to your computer) you should assess the benefits. The best known plug-in vendors will have taken the trouble to provide a certificate of authentication that will be displayed on your screen and proves that the company is who it claims and that its software is less likely to damage your computer or contain a virus.

A good example of a plug-in is the Virgin Radio Web site ('www.virgin.co.uk') that uses an audio control plug-in to let you listen to the live radio broadcasts over the Internet.

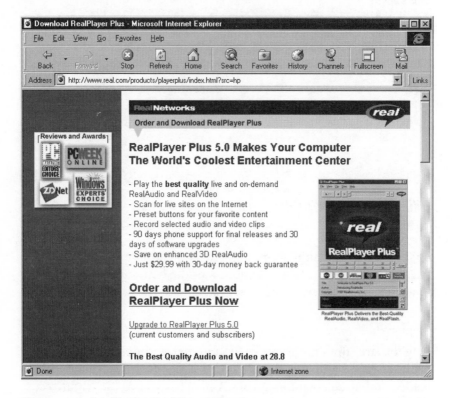

Stereo sound with the Realplayer plug-in

3

Using Electronic Mail

Electronic mail boosts productivity, improves communications and cuts costs – and that's just for starters. Once you've got your Internet link up and running, you should start thinking about electronic mail. Over the last five years, the popularity of e-mail has rocketed; in the US – land of communications – the benefits have been as welcome as a shower in the desert. With e-mail, you don't have to hold in a telephone queue, nor face an electronic voice-mail box; e-mail is faster and more reliable than the post service and you can set your mail program up so that you know exactly when your message was read.

An electronic mail program has one simple job definition – it lets you send information to another user on the Internet. You could telephone your colleague and give them the message; however an e-mail program will send as many mail messages as you like for, at most, the cost of a local phone call. There are rarely any online costs to pay on the Internet, so your only cost is the monthly fixed fee (the exception are OSLs such as CompuServe that charges for the time you are connected to the Internet).

Take the example of an international sales director who needs to brief his sales team on new products. He can telephone each salesman at their offices in each country. He could type out a memo and post this to each salesman – which would take several days by post or be expensive by courier. He could send each an e-mail message together with an image of the product and a spreadsheet to show cost and marketing spend – this would take a few minutes to deliver around the world and is free.

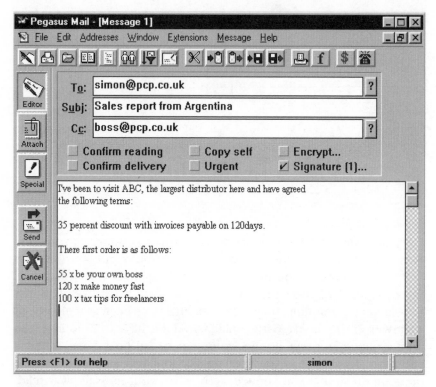

Orders flow with e-mail!

An e-mail program lets you add attachments to your mail message – literally adding any file or group of files to the message. With this, e-mail becomes a useful way of distributing data. In Microsoft Windows, you can make it a little neater and drag files into the body text of your message. Drag an Microsoft Excel file into your message and an icon appears; when the recipient double clicks on the icon, Excel starts and loads the file. You can even add voice annotations this way by including WAV objects in your mail.

So far e-mail is a great way of distributing data, but it can also be very good at giving you feedback. You can ask for a receipt of delivery: when the recipient actually opens the mail message you sent, a message is automatically sent back to you giving details of the time and date at which the message was read (invaluable for cutting office politics).

You can set up an intelligent set of rules for your e-mail system so that the software will automatically reply to messages received when you are on holiday – or forward them to another user. This is also a good technique for dealing with standard e-mail enquiries about prices. If your company has sales reps on the move, or has offices or workers abroad, it's often inconvenient and costly to keep up to date with a telephone call. With e-mail, each worker can connect to the Internet wherever they are in the world and keep up to date with the messages back at the office.

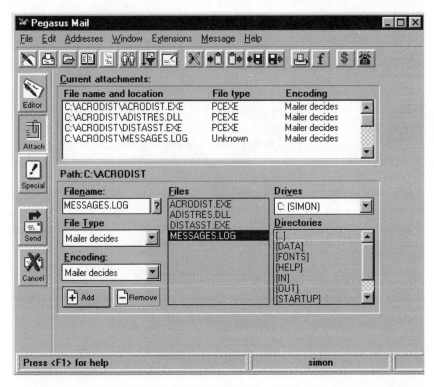

Sending files using e-mail attachments

Of course, e-mail will never get going in your company unless everyone uses it and checks their mailbox regularly. To get the ball rolling quickly, it's best to send your users on a short mail-appreciation course. The problem that many large companies soon run into is that e-mail becomes too popular and the employees spend the morning reading and replying to e-mail!

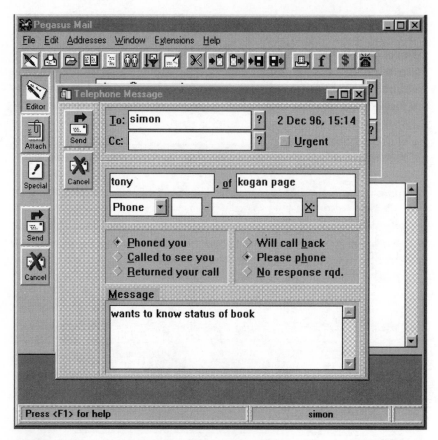

Internal office e-mail improves communication

Your mail address

Every registered user on the Internet has a unique address that is normally written in the form 'simon@pcp.co.uk'. The section to the right of the '@' sign is the company's domain name. The section to the left of the '@' sign is the user's name in that company. In my company, we have adopted the friendly approach of first names only; in larger companies it is common to see the address written as 'simon.collin @pcp.co.uk'. The one exception to this naming convention are users who are registered to the CompuServe system. CompuServe currently assigns users a number rather than a name. A typical CompuServe mail address is '10324.223@compuserve.com'. However, CompuServe does allow you to change this number to a friendlier user name, such as 'SimonCollins@compuserve.com'.

If you have just signed up to a new ISP and do not have a domain name registered for your company, then you will probably have to use the ISP's name in your e-mail address. For example, users registered to the Demon Internet service would have an e-mail address similar to 'scollin@scollin.demon.co.uk'.

For companies that want to present a unified corporate image, it's worth investing in a domain name to include on your business cards and in your electronic mail address. This feature is normally called mail forwarding and can cost up to £200 per year. This means that for a full, professional look you need an Internet account, domain name, domain name forwarding (for your Web site) and mail forwarding (for the e-mail).

To send a mail message to another user on the Internet, you will need their full e-mail address which includes their unique identifier and the domain name – as described above, this would have an '@' sign in the middle and look like 'simon@pcp.co.uk'.

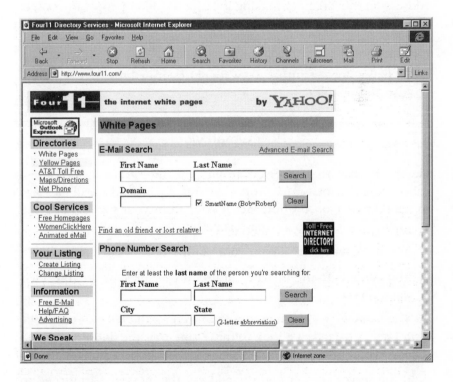

Finding another user's e-mail address

If you only have the domain name – 'pcp.co.uk' – then you cannot send me an e-mail. The one exception to this rule applies to users of OSPs including CompuServe, AOL and Delphi. These systems have an internal mail delivery and an Internet mail delivery system. This means that if you are registered with CompuServe and want to send a mail message to another user on CompuServe, you need only enter their CompuServe number. If you want to send a mail message to any user on the Internet, you need their full e-mail address.

Finding an e-mail address

Finding someone's e-mail address can be very difficult – unless you telephone them to ask for it! There are, however, several directories on the Internet that list several million users and their e-mail addresses – rather like a telephone directory. You can use these to try and find someone's e-mail address or to register your own e-mail address on the directory, making it easier for other people to contact you.

There are several e-mail address directories that will try and come up with the correct e-mail address based on any information you might have – look at 'http://www.four11.com' or 'http://www.yahoo.com/search/people/'.

How e-mail works

Electronic mail is transferred around the Internet using a system called store-and-forward. It works like this: if you send a mail message to another user on the Internet it goes from your mail box to the recipient's mail box following this path:

1. You use e-mail software on your computer to write a message.

2. You connect to the Internet and send your message to your ISP's main server.

3. The message will be temporarily stored on the ISP's server while it checks its address book to make sure that the delivery address is correct.

4. If the server doesn't find the address, the message is returned to you.

5. If the server does find the address, the server will work out the best (normally the cheapest) route across the world to get to the destination computer.

6. Your message is transferred from one server to the next until it reaches its destination.

7. Now your message has arrived at the correct server; the server looks up the recipient's name and stores the message in their postbox (this is actually just a folder or directory on the server's hard disk where incoming messages are stored).

8. The recipient still doesn't know he has received a new mail message until he next connects to his local ISP server. Once he does this, he'll be told there's a new mail message and he can finally read your note.

It's important to note that there is no permanent link between a user and his in-tray on an ISP, so he will not know that he has received a new message until he next connects to the Internet. The exception to this is for companies that have their own Internet server installed in-house and connected to their company network. In these situations, the mail would be immediately sent on to the user on the company network.

What software do I need for e-mail?

Electronic mail is one of the simplest uses of the Internet but also one of the most effective. In order to send to, and receive electronic mail from, other users on the Internet, you need to have an account with a company that provides access to the Internet – either an OSP (such as CompuServe or AOL) or an ISP (such as Demon, Pipex or Planet). In addition to the basic software that connects you to the service, you need an electronic mail application.

There are several very good e-mail software products that are available free. These let you send and receive mail, organize your messages into folders and create simple rules that automatically respond to messages that arrive at your computer. You can also use these programs to send or receive files over the Internet.

If you are using a Web browser, you will find that it should be able to manage your e-mail. For example, Netscape Communicator includes a good e-mail program and Microsoft IE includes Internet

Mail. The two main independent e-mail software products are Qualcomm Eudora ('www.qualcomm.com') and Pegasus Mail ('www.pegasus.com'). Many Internet companies supply versions of these products for new users, or you can download a copy from these Web sites using an FTP program.

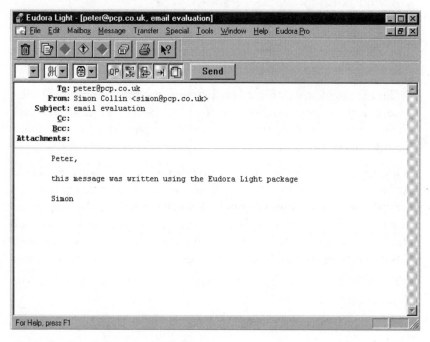

Qualcomm's Eudora e-mail software

Once you have your electronic mail program installed you need to configure it for your system. If you are using an ISP you will need to enter the address of the server computer at the ISP that manages all mail messages. This will normally be called 'post.xxx.co.uk', where 'xxx' is the name of your ISP. You will also need your user name and user password.

Sending e-mail

There are two ways to use e-mail programs – online and offline. The two modes refer to whether you are connected to the Internet whilst you type out a mail message. For example, if you have several messages to type in and send, it makes sense to type them in using your e-mail software in its offline mode (not connected to the Internet) and then dial into the Internet and send them all at once. This way saves your telephone bill. The only exception to this is for a company that has a permanent leased-line connection to the Internet and so has no telephone bills to worry about.

To send a mail message, follow these steps:

1. Start your e-mail software – elect to work offline if it gives you the option.

2. Start a new mail message.

3. Enter the recipient's full e-mail address in the 'To:' box.

4. Enter the subject in the 'Subject' box.

5. Some e-mail programs will let you send a copy of the message to another user at the same time – enter their full e-mail address in the 'CC:' box.

6. Type your message in the 'Body' section.

7. If you want to include a file, insert an attachment.

8. Select the 'Send' option.

9. The e-mail program will give you the option to dial into the Internet and send the mail.

Sending files by e-mail

Sending files via electronic mail is a very useful feature, but you might find that you come across some rather odd terms when trying to send a file. The problem lies in the way that a message is transferred: the Internet relies on text messages which uses a cut-down data packet called a seven-bit ASCII code; data files use a full ASCII code which has eight bits. If you try and send a data file over the Internet using e-mail, all of its data will become corrupted as they lose one bit. To solve the problem of the missing bit you have to UUencode the data file to turn it into a pseudo-text file that can be transmitted without problems. This doesn't sound terribly friendly – it's not. To get around this a new standard called MIME was developed that solved the problems.

Most e-mail programs now support MIME attachments (a standard that allows any type of file to be sent over the Internet and delivered correctly).

Receiving e-mail

Electronic mail messages will be stored in your account on your Internet server (located either at your ISP or in your company) until you log in and read the messages. Some e-mail programs will automatically start up and collect any new mail messages as soon as you dial into your ISP. With other programs you will have to connect to the Internet and then start the e-mail program.

When you have received a new mail message it will normally be saved into your 'Incoming' folder. Your e-mail program should be able to support several folders, which makes the job of managing your mail much easier. For example, Microsoft Exchange, part of the Windows 95 operating system, can be used to send and receive mail messages and supports folders. You can create simple rules that automatically check your new mail messages and move them into the appropriate folder – for example if it detects a product name in the subject line the software will move the mail message to a folder for this product.

E-mail with a WWW browser

As I mentioned at the start of this chapter, there are several popular e-mail application programs that will do just about everything you want. However, if you want to integrate all your Internet functions into one program, you should consider one of the new versions of Web browsers, such as Netscape Navigator 4 or Microsoft IE. These both include a built-in e-mail program that lets you send and receive mail and send and receive files using MIME attachments.

E-mail standards

There are many different standards used to send e-mail over the Internet, but the two dominant standards most commonly used are POP 3 and SMTP. These are two systems that are used to transfer mail between different servers connected to the Internet. Normally, your e-mail software will use a combination of the two standards: SMTP to send mail to your ISP and POP 3 to receive mail. (There are two different standards because SMTP is normally used to communicate between a user's computer and a post-office server and POP 3 is used to access mail stored on a post-office server.)

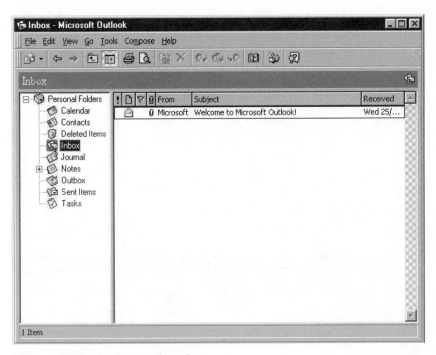

Microsoft's Outlook e-mail package

Almost all electronic mail products will use this combination of POP 3 and SMTP to send and receive messages. Check to see how your ISP delivers mail, since some ISPs do not use this combination, but instead use SMTP for both sending and receiving mail (in the UK, Demon uses this system). The advantage of using the SMTP standard for receiving mail is that you can have as many mailbox names on your computer as you want – for example 'simon', 'sales', 'info' and so on. The reason is that since the post-office server is using SMTP it thinks it is sending mail on to another post-office server rather than to a computer. If you use POP 3 to read mail – which is the system most ISPs support – then you will need to log in with a different name to collect e-mail messages for each user. Someone with an SMTP account will collect all the mail for all users at their domain when they log in.

Adding Internet e-mail to your office network

If you would like to allow all the users on your company's office network to be able to send and receive electronic mail over the Internet then you will need to set up a more sophisticated system (see also Chapter 11 for advice on setting up an Internet server).

In order to allow each user to access e-mail you will need to set up a multi-user account with your ISP. Not all ISPs are able to provide this option, so make sure that it's an option if you want to expand your Internet use later.

There are two ways of tackling the problem. The first applies to a network that already has an electronic mail system installed for local use. Typical software programs include Lotus cc:Mail and Microsoft Mail. These products let users on an office network send and receive mail. In order to allow these users to send mail outside the company you will need to buy and install a gateway program. This normally runs on its own dedicated computer and needs a link to the Internet.

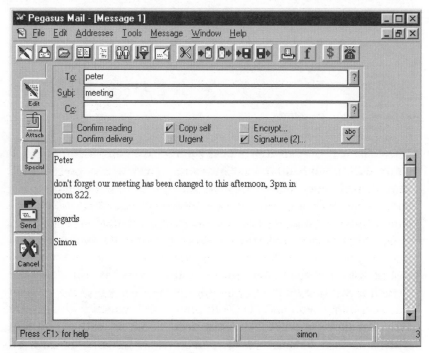

Pegasus works over local networks or the Internet

An alternative way of configuring multiple users is to provide a mail server program running on your office server. The users would run a copy of a standard Internet mail application which would store messages with the mail server program. This central software would then dial into the Internet and send messages via a multi-user Internet account set up with an ISP. Again, it's worth checking with a potential ISP before you sign up to make sure that this is possible in case you want to expand your Internet business.

Making the most of e-mail

So far, I have covered how to use electronic mail to send and receive messages and files over the Internet. This is the staple diet for e-mail systems, but you can use your e-mail software to get even more benefit from the Internet. You can subscribe to mailing lists that will automatically send you new reports, magazines or updates by electronic mail; you can even use e-mail to send commands to other computers.

Mailing lists

There are over 50,000 different mailing lists running on the Internet. These tend to be more specific than newsgroups (covered in Chapters 4 and 5) and tend also to have fewer members, so the traffic is easier to manage. The way they work is as follows. If you find there's a mailing list about drilling technology you are interested in, you send a subscription message to the list server (a piece of software that manages the mailing list). Your subscription message has to include your e-mail address which the list server will add to its internal mailing list. As soon as any member of the mailing list adds a message, it is automatically sent to every member on the mailing list. You can add messages or comment on existing messages and these too will be sent to the other members.

Before you submit a new message to a mailing list, make sure that you have looked at the FAQ (frequently asked questions) document for the mailing list. This file or message will normally tell you the rules and conditions for new messages. For example, some mailing lists might not accept any advertising, others might not accept questions on how to use a product and so on. If you ignore these conventions, you'll be flamed.

Mailing lists are a great way of keeping up to date with your particular niche in business. The problem is that with so many mailing lists available, you need to be able to find the list that's relevant to you. To solve this problem there is a directory of all the lists – visit it at 'http://www.liszt.com/'.

I have listed some of the useful mailing lists in the appendix at the end of this book – a couple of useful lists for general business are the US-based government business news which can be reached by sending an e-mail to 'email-info@financenet.gov' and the UK-based business news to which you can subscribe by sending an e-mail to 'mail-list@hm-treasury.gov.uk' with the words 'subscribe whatsnew' as the mail content. Both services will automatically send you details of new business news as it happens.

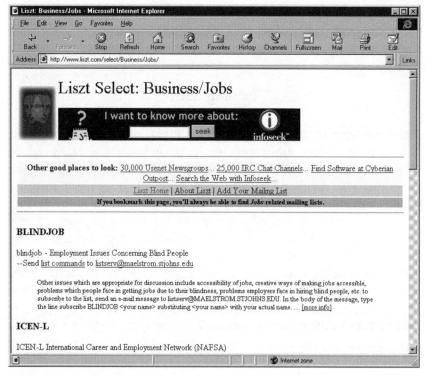

Mailing lists offer forums for discussion

For wider news coverage, try the excellent InfoBeat service ('www.infobeat.com') that will send you a daily bulletin of news stories by e-mail. You choose the topics and areas that you want to hear about and it sends a tailored 'newspaper' each morning. This service is similar to the 'push' technology channels mentioned in Chapter 4 – but you need nothing more sophisticated than an e-mail program.

Reading e-mail abroad

Electronic mail is a great benefit when you are travelling abroad. It lets you keep in touch with your office at virtually zero cost and you can read and reply to messages at any time. To read your messages you need to dial into your ISP and access your mail account. The problem with this scenario is that most ISPs tend to be confined to one country, so you normally have to make a long-distance call back to your home country, which rather defeats the object. However, there are some tricks to get around this problem.

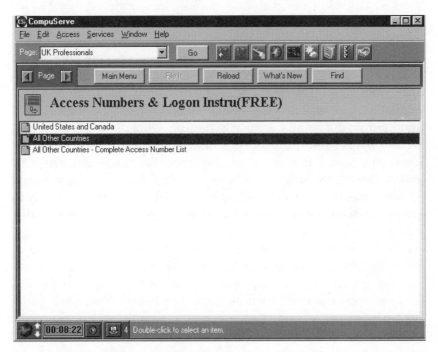

CompuServe provides local world access

The first is simple – if you are concerned more about your e-mail than other aspects of the Internet, make sure that you sign up with a worldwide provider that has local-rate access numbers around the world. These companies tend to be OSPs such as CompuServe or AOL. CompuServe has the widest network of telephone access points around the world and you can be sure of a connection wherever you are visiting.

You could set up your company Internet account to forward all e-mail to another account – such as CompuServe – which you would then use when travelling. Alternatively, there are two other systems you could use. The first is to get your e-mails automatically re-routed to a fax machine – perhaps in your hotel. There are several services that will let you do this (for example, visit 'www.gofax.com' and 'www.jfax.com').

An interesting new alternative is a service that reads out your e-mail over a telephone. It means that you can access your e-mail without using a laptop or computer; just dial the system and it reads out the text. The company charges a monthly fee for this service, but it's a cheap alternative to a laptop!

Many online companies (such as www.bigfoot.com, www.yahoo.com and www.excite.com) now provide free e-mail accounts. These can be used if you want to keep personal e-mails separate from your office network, or if you plan to travel. The disadvantage of a free e-mail account is that it cannot easily be personalized and cannot use your company's domain name. For example, you would be 'simonc@bigfoot.com' and not 'simonc@my_company.com'. The other difference is that these accounts are normally assessed using a standard Web browser rather than an e-mail program – your e-mail account will look like a Web page. This makes it easy to check your e-mail from an Internet café, or any remote computer that has access to the Web.

Another alternative is to use an Internet café or Internet terminal in a hotel. These normally only let you browse the WWW, but you can use any Internet link to read your e-mail. First, set up a free e-mail account with a service such as Bigfoot or Yahoo!. This gives you a new, free, e-mail account with a central computer. When you go off on a trip, divert your office e-mail to this new e-mail account – the mail will be stored until you read it. To read the e-mail, simply use any computer that runs a Web browser to connect to the Bigfoot or Yahoo! Web site, enter your password and you will be able to read your mail.

Some ISP companies also provide a service that allows you to read your mail using a Web browser rather than an e-mail program – without the need to set up an intermediate e-mail account as mentioned above. This means that you can read your e-mail from any Internet café or public Internet terminal. Check with your ISP to see if it supports this service (as an example, Demon UK does – 'www.demon.net').

Automatic reply service

One of uses of electronic mail is as an automatic response to sales enquiries sent by e-mail. For example, you might have set up a form on your Web page that says 'send a message to gasket@car.co.uk for more information about our range of gaskets or send a message to info@car.co.uk for information on our distributors worldwide'. Rather than having to reply to each message individually, you could set up an automatic reply system that sent a standard document about your range of gaskets to any customer that sends a message to the 'gasket' address. A customer sending mail to the more general 'info' address would get an e-mail back detailing your worldwide outlets.

There are a couple of ways to set up an automatic mail macro – sometimes called a mail robot or mailbot – which will vary according to your ISP and to the amount of mail enquiries you receive. The simplest system is based on your e-mail software running on your computer. Almost all mail software supports some form of intelligence that allows you to create rules that will analyse new mail as it is received. This is useful to move new messages into folders to keep order in your mail system, but could be used to send an 'I'm on holiday' message when you are out of the office or even to forward any mail to another user for them to deal with.

You can, just as easily, create a rule that replies to any mail sent to 'gasket' and 'info'. Now, each time you log into the Internet, the e-mail software will check for new messages and will look to check the intended recipient. Programs such as Microsoft Exchange (which is supplied with Windows 95) and office mail programs like Lotus cc:Mail provide an excellent range of functions that let you set up automatic reply systems.

The second way of creating an automated mailbot relies on your Internet server doing the work, rather than your mail software. You could create a simple program that runs on your server to send a reply to any questions from customers. If you have a server in your company, this will be a job for the programmer who will help set up your system. If you are using an ISP to host your Web site, talk to them about how you could do this. In some cases, you might find it easier to set up a simple listserver that will work in a slightly different way to normal – but again, it depends on whether your ISP will allow you to use this function.

Top tips for e-mail

1. Make sure that you read and reply to your e-mail messages at least once a day.
2. Save connection costs by composing your mail messages offline, then sending them in one batch.
3. Create a simple but effective signature file for your mail messages which includes your Web site URL.
4. Make sure that your e-mail software uses the same transfer method as your ISP!
5. Use e-mail software that supports folders (to organize your messages) and MIME (to send files).
6. Use mailing lists as a convenient way to keep up to date with trade or financial information.
7. For users that plan to travel, check you use an ISP with plenty of local access telephone numbers or use a central mail service.
8. For companies with an internal network, link your local mail software to the Internet with a gateway to let everyone send and receive mail.
9. Use automatic mailbots to reply to common queries on prices or products.
10. Set up your own mailing list to keep reps or customers informed on new developments.

4

Researching on the Internet

One of the best ways of using the Internet is to treat it as a vast research resource just waiting to be used. Many books and magazines concentrate on how to market your company on the Internet, but neglect the first stage of any product cycle or marketing campaign – research.

The Internet gives you access to libraries, government statistics, company information, product design and more. And this is not just US-based information; just about every major country has Internet connections to its public and government offices.

Unlike many other research resources, most of the information on the Internet can be accessed for free. You might be wary of information that's available free, and sometimes you should not rely on this data. For example, public, government and population statistics are normally free to access via the Internet, whereas a printed report might be difficult to obtain and you would be charged. On the other hand, information on company credit ratings or similar data is often only available if you pay for it – but again, online costs can be cheaper than a printed report.

This chapter will show you how to use the Internet to gather information for a new project or product. Sometimes you might not know what you are looking for; other times you might not know where to look. I hope that by the end of this chapter you will be able to retrieve detailed information on just about any subject matter.

Searching the Internet

The Internet is made up of thousands of individual computers, each with thousands of files and Web pages. How on earth can you hope

to find the information you are looking for? Luckily, there are electronic equivalents of a telephone directory for both files and WWW
sites that you can search online.These directories (often called search
engines) go out each day and look around the Internet for new sites.
Once they find a new site, they will check the contents and automatically create an entry for the site. If you set up your own site, it
will eventually get listed in these directories after a few weeks.
However, it's simpler to register your site manually by filling in a form
at the search engine – see Chapter 5 for more details.

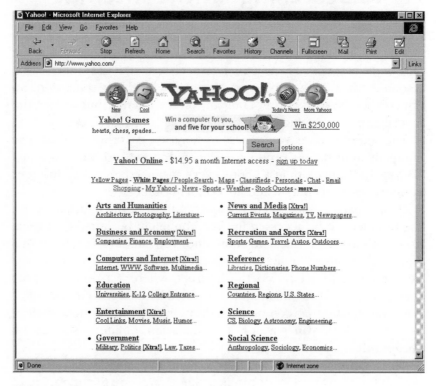

Yahoo! is one of the most popular indexes

To search for a WWW site on a subject – perhaps you want to look at
the existing market for wine suppliers – you access a search engine
and enter your key words.The main search engines are accessible via
your Web browser at 'http://www.yahoo.com' and 'http://www.altavista.
com'. There are plenty of other search engines, but these two will
point you in the right direction and provide links to the other search
engines.

Enter your key words to search for – in this case 'wine' – and click on the 'Search' button. The search engine will check its database and display the results. The information it displays is a link to the site that has information on wine, together with the first few lines of text that describes what is available at that site.

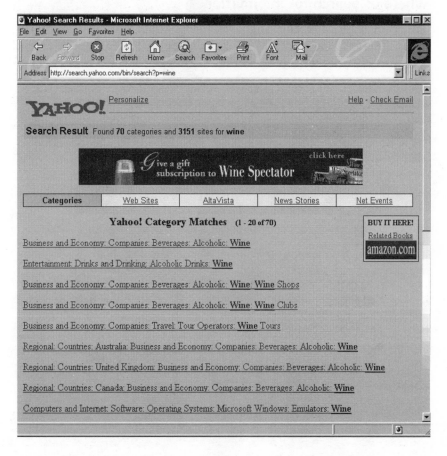

The Yahoo! search engine lists matching categories and Web sites

Tip

If your search produces hundreds of results, save the data to read offline (when you are not connected to the Internet) to save your telephone bill. Do this using the 'File/Save As' option in your Web browser to save the data as a file on your hard disk. Alternatively, create a bookmark to this page within your browser, and you can immediately get back to the page of results at any time.

To access a site that is described, click on its link (displayed in a different colour and usually underlined). Once you have had a look at the site, you can go back to the results page using the 'Back' button on your browser.

Where to search for information

There are a lot of online databases and libraries that you can use to locate the site that contains the information you need. Each of the many search engines has different benefits and most, but not all, are free to use.

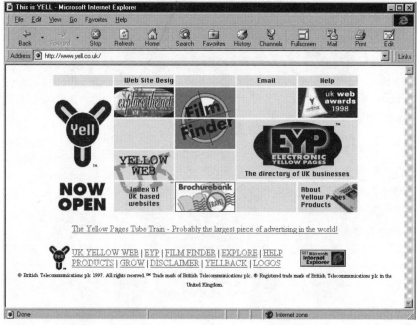

UK-specific search index

1. Yahoo! is available at 'www.yahoo.com' and is fast and comprehensive.

2. AltaVista is available at 'www.altavista.com' and provides a similar service to Yahoo!. It's worth searching both these databases, since one often pulls up extra links.

3. Yahoo! for the UK is available at 'www.yahoo.co.uk' and provides a UK-bias to Web sites. (Each country has its own version of Yahoo! – for example, 'www.yahoo.fr' for France.)

4. Lycos is at 'www.lycos.com' and provides a very comprehensive database of Web sites and FTP servers, weighted according to content. It tends to provide more information about the documents or sites than Yahoo! or AltaVista.

5. InfoSeek is at 'www.infoseek.com' and provides a vast range of libraries that cover just about every file, document and Web site on the Internet. It has a limited selection that you can access for free, or you can sign up for a charge to search every scrap of data.

6. McKinley is at 'www.mckinley.com' and has a smaller database of documents than the others. Its difference is that it rates the content carefully.

7. GOD is at 'www.god.co.uk' and provides a good range of documents, with a weighting towards UK sites.

8. YELL is at 'www.yell.co.uk' and is the electronic arm of the familiar Yellow Pages. It provides a very good database, with a strong UK emphasis.

9. If you find that the search engines return too much information (hundreds of thousands of matched documents are common for a simple search), you might prefer a search assistant such as AskJeeves (www.askjeeves.com). Type in a question in normal English and it will display a short list of possible answers – good news against information overload.

News services
If you want to keep up to date with news and reports you should take a look at the following services – the best are based in the USA but do provide some UK and European news.

1. CNN is at 'www.cnn.com' and provides an excellent site with real-time news reports, analysis, weather and more.

2. ABC is at 'www.abc.com' and provides a rival service to CNN with more emphasis on features.

3. BBC is at 'www.bbc.co.uk' and provides links to BBC programmes and news.

4. MSNBC is at 'www.msn.com' and provides up-to-date world news, with an emphasis on US news.

Newspapers

Most of the major newspapers are available in some form on the Internet. Some provide the complete text of the newspaper online, others include just news or features. These are an invaluable resource for research and for monitoring press clippings on your favourite companies.

World news from CNN

1. *The Daily Telegraph* is at 'www.telegraph.co.uk' and provides its complete text and back issues, and can be searched.

2. *The Times* is at 'www.the-times.co.uk' and provides the complete text and back issues together with special features. The entire text can be searched.

3. *The Guardian* is at 'www.guardian.co.uk' and provides a cut-down version of its text.

4. The *Evening Standard* is at 'www.standard.co.uk' and provides the text of this London evening paper.

5. The *Financial Times* is at 'www.ft.com' and provides financial news and stories and share prices.

6. The *Wall Street Journal* is at 'www.wsj.com' and provides news with a financial emphasis.

7. Reuters is at 'www.reuters.com' and provides breaking news and features from around the world.

8. The Press Association is at 'www.pa.press.net' and provides an hourly update of news headlines from around the world.

Today's news and archives from The Times

Magazines

Many magazine publishers have placed their back issues online and let you search for features and reviews. They are a good source of background material and press clippings of product reviews.

The best way to find your magazine is to search Yahoo! or AltaVista for the magazine title, which will provide the publisher's name and the address of the Web site.

User groups/newsgroups

To get an idea of what is happening in a particular area of business or education, or to judge feedback on a particular idea or new product, you should look at user groups – often called newsgroups. There are over 40,000 different newsgroups that cover a very wide range of subject areas, from children's education through to business venture capital to film and TV programmes. You can access these newsgroups using either your Web browser (if it can support this feature – which browsers such as Netscape Navigator can) or by using a separate program.

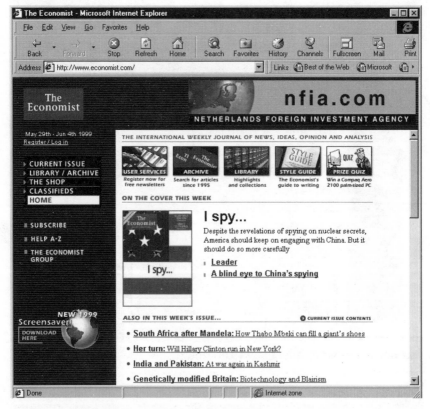

Business magazines provide useful resources

To see the range of newsgroups available (they are added to each day) enter the name of the server that manages the newsgroup feature at your ISP. (For example, if you use Demon the server is called 'news.demon.co.uk'.) Once you are connected, you will see a list of the available newsgroups. To see the messages in any newsgroup, double-click on its name and you will all the individual messages.

Messages in a newsgroup are organized in a hierarchical structure with original messages and responses to the original filed beneath it. This makes it easy to follow a particular discussion without getting lost. You can post your own message – asking if anyone knows about a subject or device that you might be researching.

There are two pieces of advice when posting a message. Don't make your message too much of an advertisement or you will get flamed (you'll receive rude messages). Secondly, do not post the same request message in lots of newsgroups (this is called spamming and you'll get rude messages in return).

Getting information with Gopher

The ways of searching for information that I have described so far really cover Web sites and documents in WWW pages. If you want to search for files stored on computers, or if you want to find other resources that are not Web pages, then you will have to resort to something called Gopher. A Gopher server keeps a list of other computers that provide documents you can search and download.

When the Internet was young and not so user-friendly, Gopher was an essential tool for searching for documents. However, almost all the information that is stored on a Gopher server is now also stored on a Web server. This means that you can access it and search it via your Web browser.

Keep up-to-date with mailing lists

Your last call for up-to-date information is a useful feature of the Internet called mailing lists or listservers. These are rather like an automated mail-shot you might send out to your customers to keep them up to date. In this case, a company has a mailing list to which you can subscribe. It will then automatically send, via e-mail, messages news of new products or events that are of interest.

To subscribe to a mailing list, you normally have to send a specific line of text to the mailing list computer on an e-mail message. There are thousands of mailing lists available: if you want a full list of all the lists available, the subjects they cover and how to subscribe, you should use your Web browser to look at the Web site 'www.liszt.net'.

5

Marketing with the Internet

The Internet provides an excellent communications tool that lets you reach tens of millions of professional users. The problem is that although this might seem like a marketing dream, you have to tread very carefully and observe the Internet rules of etiquette. If you abuse the Internet with blatant marketing or advertising, you will regret it!

This chapter will show you the ways in which you can use the Internet as a marketing and advertising medium. It will also show you how to make the most of every marketing opportunity – from signature files on electronic mail messages to product announcements in newsgroups.

Internet etiquette is very strict when it comes to commercial marketing and advertising: it's not liked. If you blunder in and do not observe these rules, you will be flamed with a barrage of rude messages from users who do not approve of your tactics. Although you might think it's worth the effort for just a few complaints, remember that if you attract too much bad publicity, you'll soon find that your Internet account has been shut down.

Marketing your Web site

Once you have designed and created your Web site, you want to make sure that as many people as possible know about it and come to visit it. The number of visitors is a good indication of how successful your Web site is and how popular it is with potential customers.

Before I cover the ways in which you can increase the visitors – or the traffic – to your Web site, it's worth thinking about the sort of visitors you want to attract and the purpose of your site. In Chapter 10,

I described the way in which you should make sure you know why you want a Web site and what you expect it to do. The design of your site will reflect your view of your company, the type of customers you expect to attract and how visitors will use the site.

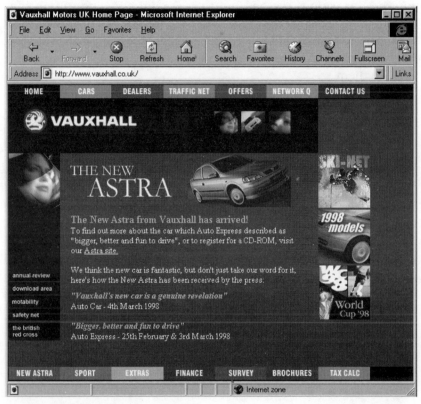

Interactive tours of new cars

For example, if you are a motor-car manufacturer, you will hardly expect any visitor to order a car over the Internet, but you might want to promote your company name and its attributes – such as build quality or price. If you are promoting a more commercial Web site that lets users order or buy goods, you want to try and increase the traffic and make sure that visitors are likely to buy.

Although it's very important to attract as many visitors as possible to your Web site, it is even more important to make sure that they are interested enough in your message to come back and visit the site another time.

Making it work

The Internet is not the place to make your millions. Anyone that tells you that you can sell your products to tens of millions of users is lying. There might well be tens of millions of users who access the Internet for various reasons, but they are not all going to buy your products. It's wise, therefore, to treat the Internet as a new marketing opportunity that should be investigated and used, but it should complement your existing advertising and marketing schemes, not replace them.

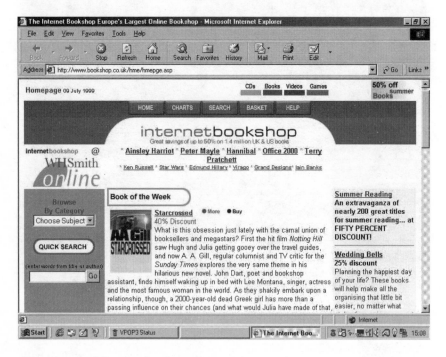

Choosing and buying books online

There are a lot of Internet marketing consultants who offer a good service, there are just as many who will provide you with a poor service. The best advice is to get an Internet account and invest some time looking at the different features: read newsgroups and look at Web sites. You can then form a good idea as to how the technology could work for your company and what type of Web site and marketing effort you want to devote to the Internet.

It can be interesting to program and design your own Web page and create marketing effort for the Internet; but with new features arriving every month, it might be wise to understand the basics and then leave the hard work to a consultant programmer who will create your Web site.

Lastly, once you have a Web site, do not forget about it! Make sure that someone in the company or marketing department has a good idea of what you want to achieve with your Internet presence and how to use the tools. They should update information on the Web site regularly and check e-mail messages at least once or better twice a day.

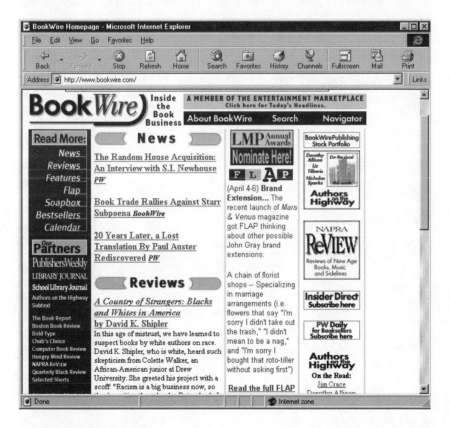

Providing industry news

Rules for effective marketing on the Internet

Provide a service

In order to attract new visitors and to keep regular visitors coming back, you need to provide the visitors with a service. The best way to ensure success is to include all the information a visitor might want, provide timely or updated information to keep them coming back, and make sure that your site is well-designed and fast to download so that they are not put off by slow speeds.

Timely information

To make sure that your site is a regular stop for visitors, make sure that you include updated and timely information about your products or services or information that might be useful to your visitors.

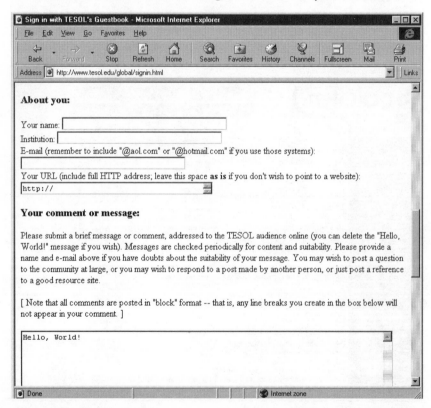

Ask visitors for feedback

Feedback

Keep the Web site interactive and try and encourage visitors to provide feedback on the service or to provide new information.

Global requirements

Make sure that you provide relevant information for your global audience. Think about how the needs of a local customer might differ from a visitor on a different continent. This can be as simple as including information on your worldwide distributors or providing pages that are translated into different languages.

Many international sites provide either different language versions of the same site, or the ability to translate the text. For example, the search engine www.altavista.com lets you instantly translate any matched page to and from a range of languages.

Depth of information

Make sure that your Web site includes a good depth of information. If you have set up an equivalent of your product catalogue, do not be surprised if visitors do not visit your site on a regular basis. If you have added value to your site and provide extra information, visitors will appreciate the effort.

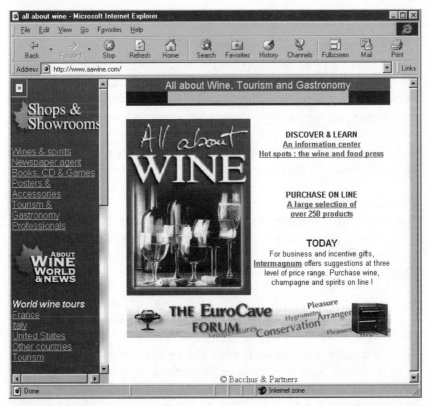

Providing depth of information

Integrate Internet marketing

Try and integrate your Web-site marketing effort and budget within the overall marketing for your company. If you are a large company, make sure that everyone in the department knows about the Web site and how it works. If you are a small company, you will find it useful to write down your marketing tasks – for traditional and Internet marketing – together with an agenda for actions, costs and results.

Participate on the Internet

One of the best forms of marketing is to go out and be heard. With the Internet this means someone should participate in newsgroups, answer e-mail messages and ensure your Web site is up to date.

Neat design

Keep the design of your Web pages neat and ensure that there are not too many large image files that would take a long time to download. For example, if you have spent a lot of effort creating a rich site you could spoil it with too many graphics that take minutes to download.

Do not abandon other channels

There are a lot of stories of companies that have made millions from the Internet, and many more stories of companies that have pulled out of the Internet. Treat the Internet as a new opportunity rather than as a replacement for existing marketing and advertising. It is not worth developing a Web site at the expense of print advertising or mail shots – these traditional marketing methods can be measured and will reach existing customers.

Consider all the options

The main front window to your company will be your Web site; however, do not forget all the other Internet opportunities to promote your company and its skills. These are described in the rest of this chapter.

Increasing the number of visitors

There are many ways of increasing the number of visitors that come to look at your Web site. Some require effort on your part, others are simple and need only forward planning. Here are the best ways you can improve the traffic to your site.

Register your Web site with search engines

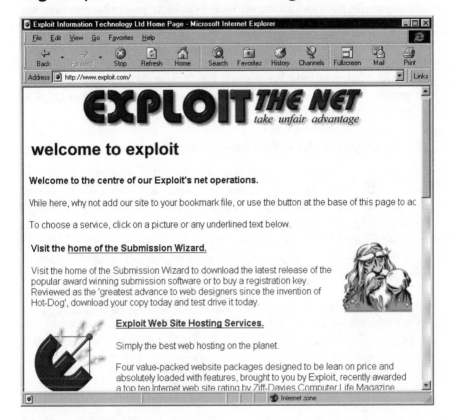

Tools to help publicize your site

Most WWW users find information by using one of the many search engines (such as Yahoo!, AltaVista or InfoSeek). All these search engines let you add your site to their index – if you don't add your site, you will not be found by users of this search engine.

There are two ways of registering your Web site with a search engine: you can visit the search engine and manually fill out an electronic registration form, or you can use an automated program to do this work for you across all the search engines. Visiting each search engine yourself takes time, but lets you enter exactly the information you want to appear on the search index. If you use an automated program to do the work, it will ask you once for short and long descriptions of your site and submit these to the search engines. You cannot then tailor the information to each index, but it does save a lot of time!

The good news about automated registration programs is that they will normally provide a free service in which your site's details are sent to a dozen of the top search engines. If you want the registration program to send the information to every search engine on the Internet, you will have to pay for this – but it's well worth the charge to ensure that your site is on each index. The two main registration programs available are located at 'http://www.exploit.com' and 'http://www.submit.com'.

Use newsgroups to reach an audience

The Usenet on the Internet is a collection of individual discussion groups called newsgroups. There are over 40,000 different newsgroups covering just about every subject you can imagine. To market your site effectively, you should look in the newsgroups that concern your product range and read the submissions. For example, if you produce language-learning reference books, you might want to look in newsgroups for each language or newsgroups for language teachers.

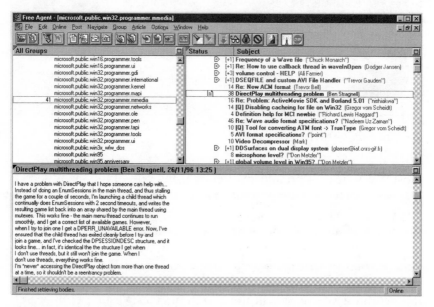

Careful use of newsgroups

Anyone can submit a new message to the newsgroup – called posting – to either reply to a previous message or to start a new subject. There is a protocol, so beware. Do not send messages to every newsgroup with a long advert about your new language tapes. This is called spamming and as a result you will receive a lot of hate mail. Instead, treat the newsgroups with respect. The best tactic is to follow the discussions and then start to add your own views or suggest your site for further information. For example, if someone asks about resources available for teachers in Peru, you might reply with a suggestion that your site has a range of language tapes, and provide the names of distributors in Peru.

Since there are 40,000 newsgroups, it might seem an impossible task to try and find ones relevant to your company. Luckily, there is an excellent guide to all the newsgroups that will list the newsgroups that cover your subject areas. To access this newsgroup guide visit 'http://www.dejanews.com'.

If you cannot find a newsgroup that covers your subject field, it might be worth setting up your own newsgroup. Talk to your ISP to see if they can help you set up and maintain a newsgroup.

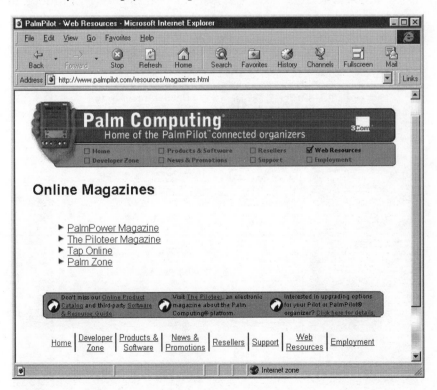

Online magazines on niche subjects

Link to related sites

Try and get a link to your Web site added to other sites that cover similar subjects. Find the sites that you think might attract similar visitors and mail the owner with your request – suggest that you add a link back to their site in return. This will provide visitors to either site a quick way to visit related sites.

If you build up enough related links you might soon find that visitors visit your Web site for this reason alone as a provider of useful links!

Swap banner advertising

A new system has been developed to allow Web sites to share banner advertising (the bars of adverts you'll often see along the top of a Web page). The scheme, called Link Exchange, will give your banner to other sites in return for you displaying other banners. It's a good way

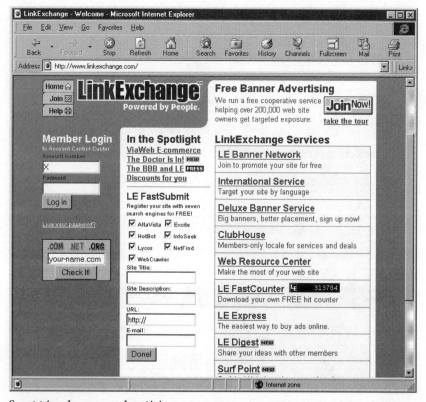

Swapping banner advertising

of promoting your site, adding interest to your site and reach a totally different set of Internet visitors. Visit the Link Exchange site at 'http://www.linkexchange.com' for further information.

Announce your Web presence

Make sure that you announce your Web site to any relevant non-Internet media. For example, send a press release to any trade magazines that cover your industry telling them that your company is now running on the Web. It's also worth sending details of your new Web site to the many Internet magazines published each month. These computer magazines normally carry a 'what's new' and 'best site' feature and might include your site if it's interesting.

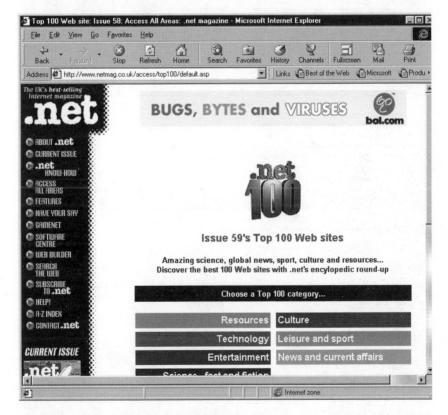

Internet magazines have top site lists

Once you have announced your Web site – together with your full URL and an e-mail address – to the press, make sure that you include your Web details in your print catalogues, business cards and on headed notepaper.

Use signature files

Almost every electronic mail program lets you create a signature file. This is normally a few lines (more than eight is considered pushy) of text with your name, company, contact details and maybe your company's slogan. The signature file is automatically added to the end of any e-mail message you send and provides a good company advert.

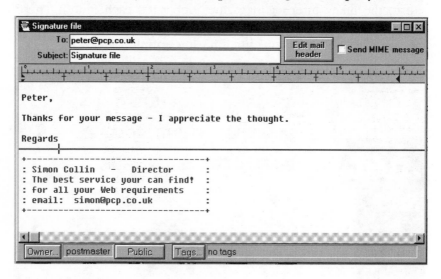

E-mail signatures reinforce a message

You should also create a similar signature file to use with your newsgroup browser so that it will automatically add your contact details to any message you post to a newsgroup.

Provide something for the visitor

Your site has to compete with millions of other sites, so make sure that there's something useful for the visitor. One of the popular features of a good Web site is the ability to download useful files – programs, documents and databases. Why not store some useful files on your Web site and allow visitors to download these? For example, a language-learning tape publisher could store a section of the audio tape as a sound file which users could download to try out the product. They might also provide other related files – including shareware

- for, say translation, dictionaries or language games. To include share-ware files on your Web site, check with the author to make sure he does not mind.

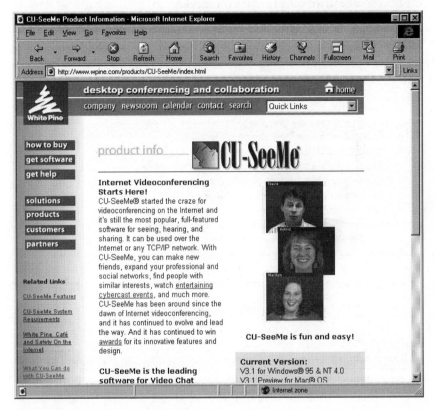

Video conferencing over the Internet

Select an effective domain name

The first thing any user will have to do is to enter your full Internet address - called your URL. This will include your domain name and will read something similar to 'www.microsoft.com' for Microsoft. Try and make your domain name as intuitive as possible. Do not make it complex or too clever - remember that the visitors will be from around the world so a pun might not work in each language. If you register your own domain name, you have a choice of endings: for example, '.co.uk' indicates that a company is based in the UK. If you want your company to appear global you could register the '.com' ending which is normally used by companies in the USA. Lastly, do not forget about the language difference between UK and USA English: a good Web site called 'colour-prints' offering cheap photography would not work in the USA and leaves a competitor open to register 'color-prints' and steal your audience.

Marketing plan for the Internet

1.   Register your domain name.
2.   Look at the Internet and decide your approach.
3.   Design and create a Web site.
4.   Announce the new Web site to trade journals.
5.   Register your Web site with search engines.
6.   Submit your Web site to computer magazine reviews.
7.   Include your Web URL address in company stationery.
8.   Create a signature for e-mail and newsgroups.
9.   Find relevant newsgroups.
10.   Spend time reading and participating in newsgroups.
11.   Look at alternative marketing schemes such as banner swaps and link swaps.
12.   Make sure you keep your Web site updated and that you reply to mail messages.

Measuring your success

One of the important points of any marketing campaign is its success rate. You might think that it's difficult to measure success on the Internet, since there are few ways to see your users. Luckily, there are several ways to measure the traffic to your site and the number of visitors.

One of the most popular schemes around at the moment is to add a visitor counter to your Web site. It reads something similar to 'you are visitor nnn', and is incremented with each new visitor to your site. There are several ways to include a counter – described in Chapter 10 on Web design and Chapter 11 on server installations.

The second way of measuring traffic is to look at your server access logs. If you have your own in-house Internet server, the server software will keep a file that records the Internet address of each visitor and the Web page or image they looked at. If you are using an ISP to host your Web page, make sure that they can provide access logs – your effort will be impossible to measure without these logs.

Each line in an access log records a 'hit'. A hit is recorded each time a user looks at a different Web page, opens a graphic image or downloads a file. As you can imagine, if one user looks at four or five pages, each with several images, that one user will record 10 or 20 hits in your access log.

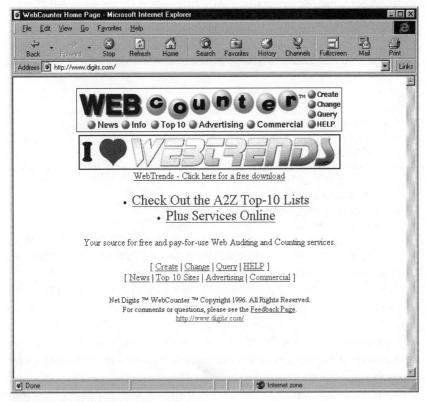

Using a third-party access counter

A hit is very useful in telling you which parts of your Web site are popular. Each line in the access log provides the address of the visitor and the Web page visited, so it's relatively easy to see if a new Web page is proving popular or to check the response to a special offer advertised on a particular page.

Tip

Visitor counters can be deceptive – ignore the total number of hits you receive and the number of hits advertised on other sites. Instead, concentrate on individual visitors, how they browse the site and their country of origin.

The access logs are stored as plain text files that can be downloaded from your ISP (using FTP) and opened in any word processor. They are normally arranged by time and date. To see how many individuals have actually visited your site, you would need to count the different user addresses that appear in the access logs – or use a visitor counter.

Tip

If you have just published your Web site put the visitor counter on a page that only you know about, but refer it to your Web site's 'index.html' page to record the visitors to your contents page. This prevents the embarrassment in the first few days of your counter reading 'you are visitor three'.

Analysing access logs

It is worth spending some time at the end of each week looking at your access logs. The number at the start of each line provides the unique address of the visitor, but you cannot use this to e-mail them, since many addresses are assigned randomly and change each time the visitor connects to the Internet. The parts of the address that do **not** change are the country of origin of the visitor. There are several utility programs on the Internet (use 'www.yahoo.com' to search for access logs) that will analyse your access logs and list the visitors by country.

Some Web browsers store information on the previous site that your visitors have looked at. If you use a little CGI script to query the visitor, it's possible to find out where they visited before they arrived at your site (see Chapter 7 for more details on CGI! This is a useful tool to check if there is a common point for the majority of the visitors. Perhaps they all see your site on one particular search engine – in which case, check your entries on the others. If they all visit another commercial site before yours, why not contact that site and suggest an advertising banner?

Lastly, try and encourage visitors to sign a guest book. This could give them entry to a prize draw or something similar. There are several scripts available that let you create a guest book (see Chapter 7 for information on Perl scripts).

6

E-commerce: Shopping and Payment

One of the boom sectors of the Internet has been its use as an online shop, allowing visitors to choose products and pay for them online. This sector, normally called e-commerce, ties together several different technologies, including banking (authenticating a credit card), programming (a database of products) and Web design (the Web site that is displayed to the user). However, thanks to improved design, it is now straightforward to set up and configure an online shop, and it's even possible to open a shop within a few days – ready to accept the first orders!

Just a few years ago, when the first shops were set up on the Internet, the effort required to install and configure different parts of the puzzle was huge – enough to put off anyone with hopes for a new outlet channel. You would need a programmer, Web designer and e-commerce specialist to help you navigate the links between Web page, database, credit card company and delivery system. Thankfully, everything has changed within the past six months – and, at its simplest, you could even start selling a few products on the Web, for free, with just a few mouse clicks.

Setting up a shop

There are many business advantages to setting up a shop on the Internet.

Your Web site provides a good way to market your products and services to a potentially vast audience of international customers – an

Internet shop can make it easier for them to purchase your range of products, especially if you have no local distributor.

An Internet shop provides a new outlet that stocks all your products and is open 24 hours per day.

After the initial set-up process, your Internet shop provides a very efficient selling operation, with low running costs, no rent and no employees needed to staff it. Stock can be purchased just in time, according to the flow of orders, releasing cash. If your company sells information, such as a database or industry news, you can allow the customer to buy the product from your Internet shop, and then also deliver the product directly to the customer. This is used to good effect by software companies that offer a discount on products purchased over the Internet – after all, it saves the company manufacturing, shipping and distribution costs.

Once your customers start to use your Internet shop, you will find it easier to track each customer's buying habits – software can give you an insight into the ways your customers buy your products, and

Online shops provide a new outlet that's convenient for consumers and retailers

can also help customers. For example, many Internet shops store a customer's address details and favourite products to make re-ordering quick and easy.

Your Internet shop can attract a new customer base and provide better service for existing customers, but careful planning is needed before you start to set it up.

What sells over the Internet?

At the start of this new consumer revolution, the products that sold best over the Internet were those that appealed most to the original core Internet audience of 18–30-year-old affluent men. The first Internet shops sold books, software and computer products. These matched the Internet's unique ability to include thousands of products in the virtual store, yet with no need for initial stock!

Books are a great example: consumers want to be able to find a specific title quickly or browse through categories of subjects – they want as much choice as possible. As a product, books need no expert backup or support and can be shipped easily around the world. Companies such as Amazon (www.amazon.com) were founded by linking a vast database of titles to a good search system and an effective order and shipping warehouse.

Leisure products

Some of the best products to sell are consumer leisure products. Since Internet users are still dominated by young (18–30) men with a relatively high disposable income, successful shops stock software and computer equipment, books and music CDs. Many online shops (including the major booksellers, such as Amazon and Barnes and Noble (www.barnesandnoble.com)) now allow customers to add their own reviews to products that are listed – this means products that are normally bought by recommendation, such as books, wine and software, sell well.

Niche products

The Internet makes it easy to find the most specialist sites and this is another market opportunity. If you sell a range of standard goods available in any high street, then potential consumers will have no problem finding the goods. However, if you have a specialist product, from handmade cheese to antique watches, you are more likely to see growth by setting up an Internet shop.

If consumers want to buy a special type of cheese or wine, they might not know where to start. If they search on the Internet, they could come across your site, making shopping for exotic goods very easy. For example, local regional products (such as cheese, crafts, or drink) all sell well to an export market via Internet shops. These customers would be impossible to target in any other way. Exotic products not available on the high street (such as organic meat and vegetables) are easy to buy using the Internet.

Information

If your company offers a specialist skill or trades on its knowledge (for example, lawyers, architects, or stockbrokers), you could sell this information over the Internet – albeit in a different way to a standard product. For example, if you supply instant share prices, this can be published on the Internet and users charged for access. Companies that publish information-rich magazines and journals have discovered that the Internet is a new and effective sales channel. For example, *AutoTrader*, the weekly classified advertising magazine covering cars for sale (www.autotrader.com), publishes all of its advertisements direct to its Web site. Potential customers can search the site for free – in this model, revenue is generated from the people placing advertisements.

Setting up your shop

Setting up a major new Internet shop – on the scale of an Amazon.com – is very expensive in time, technology and expertise. However, not many of these mammoth sites are launched – instead the growth has been in smaller businesses launching their own specialist Internet shop. In this case, set-up costs are low; in some cases, specialist commerce Internet providers will even provide small sites for free to encourage diversity (the commerce division of Yahoo! (store.yahoo.com) will provide a free site for anyone selling fewer than 10 products).

To set up your Internet shop you will need specialist commerce software that mimics all the traditional shop features, including organizing the range of products, tracking orders, and processing payments. This software, normally called shopping cart software, also lets users choose products as they browse your catalogue, adding them to a virtual shopping basket. Just as in a real shop, the customer can then move to the checkout counter to pay for all the goods.

Some e-commerce providers let you test the water by creating a working shop, for free!

The shopping cart software manages the basic functions of your shop, but it does not handle the banking side of the transaction. For example, almost all shopping baskets can ask shoppers for their method of payment (credit card, e-cash) and record the card number. To provide real-time credit card clearance, you will need to link the shopping cart software to a specialist clearing agency – via the Internet.

The key to the system lies in the effectiveness of the shopping cart software. There are dozens of different products available; some are free, others can be purchased for a one-off charge, others still are charged on a monthly rental or percentage basis.

Small shops will find the simplest way to set up a shop is to use one of the low-cost products from a large specialist supplier. These normally need no programming; just enter the details of your products. The biggest suppliers include the commerce arm of Yahoo! (store.yahoo.com and www.icat.com). Small sites with just a few products are often free, you do not need to install any software and your site takes just a couple of hours to go live. The shop pages actually reside on the supplier's Web site, so you will have two separate locations for your main Web site and your shop – not a problem, but it can be difficult to design shops in this way.

Any other size shop or those that need flexibility will need to install software on their Web server. If you rent Web space from an Internet service provider, ask if they have a pre-configured shopping cart package. It might be a chargeable extra, but it will save you days of valuable time configuring the software. You might also need to set up a link to a specialist clearing agency to process payments (see below) and you will certainly need to set up a secure section of your server (see page 90) to allow users to be confident about entering credit card details.

Set-up costs for your shop will vary, according to your requirements and Internet service provider. However, you will probably have to pay an extra monthly fee to maintain a secure section of your Web site to allow users to enter credit card details safely. You will also have to purchase or rent the shopping cart software and you will need to pay for credit card processing and bank charges.

Banking

If a customer wants to buy your products, the background scenario might run as follows: the customer finds the products using the search feature of the shopping cart, and the products are added to their virtual shopping basket until they are ready to pay. The shopping cart software asks the user for their credit card number and automatically (and securely) passes this information on to a specialist clearing agency. The agency checks that the credit card is valid and debits the customer's card on your behalf. This process takes around 10–30 seconds, after which the customer is told that their order has been processed.

If you want to accept credit card payments, you will need a merchant bank account (supplied by your bank) that allows you to accept payments via credit card, or you can use the clearing agency to handle this on your behalf – there is normally an extra charge for this.

If you would like to process the credit card automatically in real time (rather than manually telephone through the card details yourself) you will also need an account with a specialist clearing agency that can handle real-time credit card clearance. Companies that provide this service include www.netbanx.co.uk and www.worldpay.com.

Payment on the Internet

One of the problems that has always dogged the Internet is how to pay for goods advertised on it. There are now several systems available that make it feasible for both users and electronic retailers to buy and sell over the Internet.

The problem has always been one of security. The crux of the matter lies in the fact that electronic mail messages are normally sent unencrypted. That's to say, anyone who intercepts your electronic mail message could read its contents without difficulty. There has been a reluctance by users to send their credit card details in an electronic mail message that could be read by any other user. Worse, since you don't actually know whether a retailer exists outside the Internet, it's a brave person who orders sight unseen to an unknown company via an insecure message.

The reality is rather different. Yes, electronic mail messages could be read by anyone who happens to intercept the message, but the chances of this happening are slim. There are millions of electronic mail messages being transmitted every hour – why would a fraudster pick yours? It's rather like giving your credit card details over the telephone; someone could be listening in or bugging your phone, but the chances are remote.

However slim the chances of fraud it's a problem that had to be resolved before the Internet would be taken seriously by industry and get the confidence vote from the customer who would eventually order over it. There are many different ways of creating a secure payment system on the Internet that would be suitable for very different products:

● *standard credit card*. The details are entered on a secure site that scrambles the information before transferring it over the Internet to the bank.

● *virtual credit card*. The user sets up an account with an Internet bank that provides a secure channel for payment of goods.

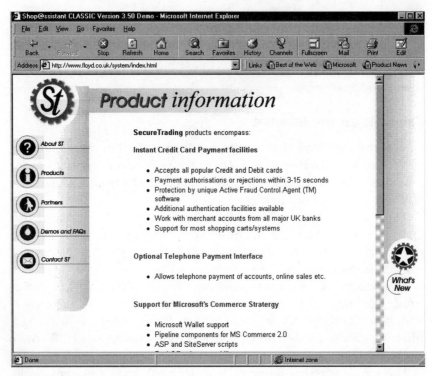

Using a specialist e-commerce provider to support instant, online credit card processing

- *virtual tokens.* The user buys credit at an Internet bank and receives electronic tokens in return. These tokens can then be used to buy products.

- *organized billing or direct debit.* The user submits an electronic mail to the vendor who then contacts them by telephone or fax to ask for their credit card details.

- *encrypted mail messages.* A user sends an order with credit card details via an encrypted mail message, which only the vendor can decrypt. This typically uses the popular PGP technology.

The most common set-up is the first in the list – the customer uses a standard credit card and enters the details in a secure Web site. This site encrypts any information sent over the Internet (from the user's computer to the server), ensuring that the card details cannot be read by a hacker. Customers are now used to this type of set-up and, generally, trust it. The technology most often used to provide this secure Web site is called SSL (secure socket layer).

There is a range of payment processing systems available; each has its benefits and drawbacks. Some simply process a standard credit card, others require the customer to create a new online bank account. Choosing the correct processing system will depend on your goods and the type of customer that will be visiting your site.

First Virtual

This is a virtual bank that is part of the First USA Bank. The bank lets you set up a real account with it. You then tell the bank how you would like to pay for goods you buy over the Internet – either charged to your credit card or debited from your account. You give these instructions by letter or by telephone. Next, you give the bank an authorization phrase and it issues you with a pseudo credit card number. Now, if you want to buy goods over the Internet, just give the vendor your pseudo credit card number at First Virtual and e-mail First Virtual confirmation, together with your authorization phrase. That's it. There is no encryption or special software. The only drawback is that you cannot use this system to buy goods, you can only use it for information. Further information is available at www.fv.com.

CheckFree

CheckFree has teamed up with another company, called CyberCash, to offer a secure digital wallet that is stored on the customer's computer. This technology has been bought by CompuServe to allow any of CompuServe's customers to buy goods over the Internet.

Commerce Net

Commerce Net was formed from VeriFone (a major point-of-sale supplier) and EIT, who developed the S-HTTP system. Further details of the state of this system can be found at www.commerce.com.

DigiCash

DigiCash is an unusual system in that it lets you pay for goods anonymously – just like normal cash. The customer and the vendor require special software. The customer has a special digital signature that authenticates a sale and the vendor can then prove that the customer has paid for the goods. Further information is available at www.digicash.com.

Netbanx

Netbanx is a company that provides a range of merchant services for companies that want to trade on the Internet. Visit them at www.netbanx.com.

VeriSign

VeriSign provides a range of secure Web services; it acts as an independent certification agency (for SSL) and provides payment options and links to banks. Visit them at www.verisign.com.

SET and credit cards

The most popular way of paying for goods and information over the Internet is probably by using a credit card. Many of the other secure schemes discussed later in this section try to provide a secure and private means for customers to send their credit card details to the vendor. To try and get around the problems, the two major credit card companies – Visa and MasterCard – have got together and produced a new system called SET (secure electronic transactions).

The SET technology is now developed and addresses most of the main concerns of paying by credit card over the Internet. These are:

- privacy – to assure customers that their credit card details will not be read by another user;

- integrity – to ensure that the details sent by the customer are received correctly by the vendor and have not and cannot be changed;

- user authentication – to provide proof that the customer really is the legitimate holder of the credit card;

- vendor authentication – to provide proof that the vendor is authorized to accept payments by credit card.

SET is, in practice, not quite up and running. To get further information, look at the Visa and MasterCard WWW sites at www.visa.com and www.mastercard.com.

Secure Web sites

A secure Web site was seen as the best solution to the problem of how to send credit card details over the Internet. It works as follows:

when a user looks at a normal Web page, the remote Web server sends the page of text and images together with the formatting codes over the Internet. All the information travelling between the user and the remote site (over the Internet) is in plain text – if you could intercept it, you could read it.

When a user looks at a secure Web page, his or her browser and the remote Web server exchange security details and work out a unique encryption scheme. The remote Web server then uses this encryption scheme to encrypt the normal Web formatting commands before sending these to the user's browser, which then decrypts them and displays the page. When the browser sends information back (such as a credit card number) this too is encrypted. All the information travelling between the user and the remote site (over the Internet) is encrypted – if you could intercept it, you could not read it.

There are several different technologies that can provide secure Web site pages. The most common is called SSL (secure sockets layer). It is supported by special software that runs on your Web server (or the Web server of your ISP). The system automatically creates a secure link between the user and the server that encrypts any information sent via this link. For example, the Netscape Navigator browser normally has a broken key in the bottom left-hand corner. This indicates whether or not the browser is connected to a plain Web server that is not secure. If you do connect to a secure Web server, Navigator changes this key icon so that the key appears whole – you can now be sure that any information transferred is secure.

Authentication

There is one problem left that causes a lot of headaches on the Internet. Assume that you visit a secure Web site and that you can type in your credit card number safe in the knowledge that the card details cannot be read by anyone else. The problem is this: how do you know that the company running the secure Web site is what it claims to be?

The Internet is not like the high street – you cannot walk into a physical shop, look around, ask to meet the manager and use your experience to decide if the company is reputable. On the Internet, anyone can set up a secure Web site, call him or herself by a well-known name, and start trading. There are laws against this, but by the time you had brought a lawsuit the damage would have been done, and customers might have used their credit cards to buy goods.

The answer is called authentication. The company running the shop has to prove to an independent body that it is who it claims to be; the independent body issues them with a certificate and this is stored on its Web site. When you visit its Web site, this certificate is automatically displayed to prove authenticity.

If you are a customer, make sure that before you shop at a Web site, it has these two features: it is a secure Web site that encrypts all information and it has a certificate of authentication.

If you are a business and want to set up a reputable shop on the Internet, you will need a secure server and you will need to apply for a certificate of authentication (one of the most popular companies issuing certificates is called VeriSign – www.verisign.com).

Encryption on the Internet

Earlier in this chapter, I mentioned how a secure server uses a system to encrypt all the information that travels between the customer and the server. The two most common secure server standards are called SSL and S-HTTP. These are described below.

An alternative to a secure server is to use e-mail ordering. This might be useful for small companies that expect low volume orders, or who just want to test the waters before committing to a complex and expensive secure server. Customers send an e-mail with their order and credit card, but instead of sending a plain text message they use an encryption system to scramble the text so that only they and the vendor can read the information. One of the best-known e-mail encryption systems that can be used for this set-up is called PGP (pretty good privacy).

PGP

PGP is a system that has caused all sorts of problems regarding freedom of speech in the United States. It provides a simple public key encryption system that works as follows. You, the vendor, want to sell goods over the Internet. You install PGP and create a public key for your company. You publish this public key on your Web site. Now, if customers want to send their credit card details they use your unique public key from your Web site with the PGP software to encrypt their credit card. They send this back to the vendor. The vendor created the public key and is the only person who can decrypt the message from the customer. The problem with PGP is that government agencies found it too difficult to crack. Because of this they insisted that it could only be used outside the United States in a less secure form. It is, however, still useful for simple credit card sales.

Creating a secure Web site

I defined the various methods available to create a secure Web site earlier in this chapter, but in practice there are two main secure systems in use on the Internet, which provide slightly different solutions: S-HTTP from the NCSA and Netscape's SSL. Both provide a way of encrypting information as it passes from the user's computer to the remote Web server – over the potentially dangerous public Internet.

If you want to provide a secure Web site that lets users enter credit card or other details within a Web form without risk, and you want to set up a system now, then either S-HTTP or SSL will work and are offered by a number of different companies (although SSL probably has the bigger market share).

It is worth noting that S-HTTP will only provide secure Web pages. SSL can secure your Web pages and also FTP or Telnet sessions to allow users to download files in a secure manner (see Chapter 2 for more information on FTP and Telnet).

S-HTTP

S-HTTP is a secure version of the standard protocol used by a Web browser to communicate with a Web site and was developed by the NCSA (who also developed the concept of the Web). Its great advantage is that it is not a proprietary standard but, although supported by almost every Web server's software, it is not so well supported by commercial Web browsers. However, Netscape (which produces the rival SSL secure protocol) has said that it will try and include support for S-HTTP within its products in the near future. Once this happens, a user will be able to use a browser to communicate with either an S-HTTP or SSL server.

SSL

The second and dominant standard used for secure HTTP sessions is SSL (secure sockets layer) and was developed by Netscape. Like S-HTTP, this standard is included in just about every commercial Web server product aimed at online business users. SSL has the great advantage in that it is also directly supported by the Netscape and Microsoft IE Web browsers (the status of the session is indicated by the key icon in the lower left corner of the screen: a broken key is a connection to an unsecure server, a full key shows a session to a secure SSL server).

Implementing SSL on your Web site

Since SSL is the current dominant standard used to secure Web sites, I will describe how to use SSL for your site, but S-HTTP is not too different. To implement a secure Web site you must either have your own Web server or use an ISP (Internet service provider) which provides SSL as an option. For example, Demon does not yet provide this option, but Planet does. If you are modifying your own Web server, check that it supports SSL – almost all of the main commercial server products do support this standard or have optional plug-ins that provide SSL functionality. If you are using an ISP, call and give them notice that you want to use the SSL feature (if it is supported, it's often a chargeable extra).

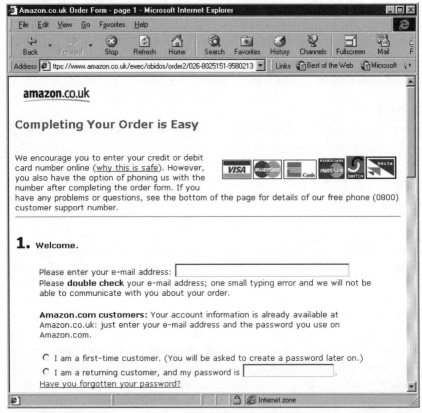

Any online shop should provide a secure site to allow users to enter credit card details

In order to set up SSL on your server you will first have to create a digital certificate for your server that will then be used by the software to create the public user keys and to authenticate the server to any user who asks. Once you have generated a digital certificate, you will need to have it authenticated by an independent organization (see below). In return you get an authenticated certificate that is used by the SSL software for all other operations.

The steps to configuring SSL on almost any Web server are:

● generate the initial encryption key pair and the request for an authentication certificate (the SSL management software will do this);

● request an authenticated certificate from a Certification Authority organization (contact a company such as VeriSign);

● install the authenticated certificate on your server (a simple step using the SSL management software);

● start the SSL software with the authenticated information (again, a simple step).

The second step, requesting an authenticated certificate, is not complex. You should use one of the many Certification Authorities on the Internet, which will process your request. One of the most popular organizations is called VeriSign (www.verisign.com). Some Web server products, such as Microsoft's IIS Web server, include utilities to help you manage new keys and certificates. In IIS, use the Key Manager utility to generate a request file that can then be sent to the Certifier.

Solutions

If you want to set up a shop on the Internet that allows customers to buy your products, you will have to set up a secure system that enables your customers to pay with confidence. As you have discovered, there are ways of providing this security and many ways of processing their orders, but not all are ideal. While you wait for the technology to catch up you could be losing sales, so it is important to get a system up and working today.

Electronic shopping malls

An Internet user who wants to buy a product on the Internet can either go to a shop set up by a company or, for more choice, can visit an electronic shopping mall. These malls have many different companies located within the confines of one site. A visitor can select products from any of the companies and pay for all of them at one central checkout point. One of the best examples of this technique is the site provided by Barclays Bank – www.barclaysquare.co.uk. This site gathers together a series of shop sites and lets you look at products and, finally, buy them with the Barclays secure payment scheme. If you have a shop service that you think would work better in a mall site, you should visit the malls and see how they work and how they are supported. It can be more expensive to set up a site on a mall than on an individual site. However, with the publicity malls get, you can be sure of far more traffic and visitors.

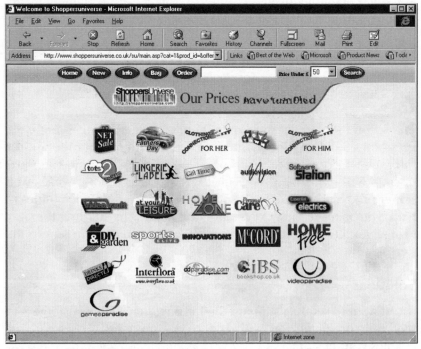

ShoppersUniverse provides a comprehensive and friendly mall

Your shopping site

Shopping malls provide a good solution for some companies, but you might prefer the flexibility and freedom offered by designing and installing your own shop site. There are several practical solutions that offer flexibility and ease of use to your customers.

For the most flexible approach, ideal for complex or custom

shopping sites or where real-time credit card processing and a large number of items are stocked, you should consider working with your ISP to set up your own shopping cart and payment system. Although there are several steps, and the initial costs are high, the process is straightforward and the running costs very low:

1. Register your domain name.

2. Ask your ISP to set up a secure server using SSL (the most common security system).

3. Apply for a certificate of authentication from VeriSign – you will need your company papers.

4. If you want payment by credit card, apply for a merchant account from your bank.

5. If you need to process credit card payments in real time, contact a specialist clearing company.

6. Select and install a shopping cart software program.

7. Market your new Internet shop.

Customers with a smaller inventory of products or who do not need real-time card processing – or simply do not want the bother of setting up the different parts of the previous system – should look to a turnkey solution from a large commerce provider (such as shop.yahoo.com or www.icat.com):

1 Register your domain name.

2. Design your main site.

3. Apply online for a new shop site at a commerce provider and pay a monthly fee for the service.

4. Use the online tools to design your shop pages, adding images, text, prices and so on.

5. Add links from your main site to the new shopping site.

6. Orders will be sent to you by encrypted e-mail, or they can be downloaded from a secure site.

7. Process the orders in-house and carry out any credit card transactions manually.

Delivering Product via the Internet

One of the problems of the Internet is that it's always been difficult to imagine how to deliver a product to a customer. Over the past years, companies have come up with ingenious ways of automating the entire shopping experience. Not only can a customer browse your online catalogue, but they can then order a product and pay for it securely over the Internet. The one last link to a business on the Internet is how to deliver the product to the purchaser.

This chapter is not going to explain a new exciting way of sending a shiny bicycle over the Internet, but it will provide some pointers to show you how companies are making the most of the Internet to deliver their products.

Delivering information-based products has always been relatively easy. If you want to send the contents of a book, magazine or journal over the Internet then it's easy to convert them to a text file or formatted document and let the customer download a copy to his computer. The same applies to software companies that let users download the software they have just bought. Not only is it instant access for the customer, but it saves money in packaging, printing and mailing the 'real' product.

Delivering electronic products

I'll start with this section because it's the easiest! It will also show you the various ways in which you can interact with your customers and might give you ideas of how you might adapt the technology for your own use.

Once you have your product stored as a file on your computer, you can send it to any other user over the Internet. For example, you

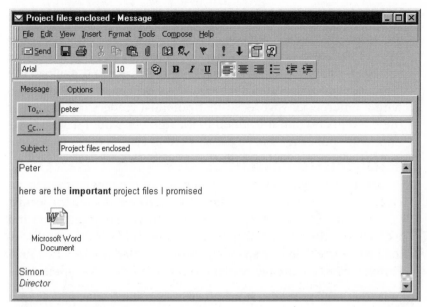

Sending updates and files by e-mail

might have files that contain documents, a spreadsheet or the design of a new component. If you want any user to have access to a file, you would store it on the Internet server that you use. If you want to be selective about the people that can access the file, you could either store it on the Internet server and protect it with special access controls, or you could keep it on your own computer and send it to particular users.

● A software publisher has all its products stored as files. When it produces a new program it wants to sell, it could store the program files on its Internet server and charge users that want to download the files. This would save on the production costs of producing CD ROMs, printing manuals and mailing the product to the customer.

● A journal publisher could save the next issue of its monthly journal to a document file which would be stored on its Internet server. Subscribers would be able to enter their user name and password and read the electronic version of the journal. This would save the publisher the printing and mailing costs. To add benefit for the subscriber, the publisher might store all the back issues of the journal online, providing a library that subscribers could search.

● An academic book publisher could save the next publication as an electronic document - such as in Adobe Acrobat format (see pages 112-13 for more details). The publisher would store the electronic book on its Internet server and allow any user to download the book. However, the publisher would protect individual chapters with a different password, so that potential readers could look at the contents list and introduction for free but would have to telephone the publisher and pay with a credit card in order to receive the passwords for each chapter.

● A newspaper could produce a summary of the news stored as an electronic document (again, the Adobe Acrobat document format is useful since it can be read by almost any type of computer) and would store this on its Internet server so that anyone could download it for free. The newspaper publisher would use this as a marketing tool to encourage readers to buy the full newspaper.

● A DIY company might store all of its product information in a glossy multimedia version of its catalogue. This would allow buyers to search for all types of hammer or electric drill – and view pictures of the items. To promote its services, the DIY company would store this multimedia file on its Internet server and allow any potential customer to download the file so that they can search for tools in the comfort of their own home. This is a crossover application in that it's using an electronic file to sell real products.

Delivering real products

The previous examples might be obvious examples and well suited to the Internet. After all, it's easy to transfer electronic files over an electronic communications channel. But what about all the thousands of other industries that do not create software, or publish academic books and journals? Here you need some lateral thinking to give the potential customer everything he wants – except the final product. Make it as easy as possible for the customer to learn about the product and so encourage him to order it.

● One large 'virtual' bookshop lists almost every single book in print. A customer can select a book that matches his criteria and the bookshop computer can be programmed to learn about a customer's reading habits. The customer would be able to view the book jacket, read reviews of the book and perhaps see the contents (all this information is supplied to the bookshop by the publisher). The customer can then order the book. The virtual bookshop takes the order and passes it automatically to a linked warehouse that supplies the book from a small stock, or, with some booksellers, it is passed to a local specialist wholesaler.

● A wine merchant includes tasting notes for all the fine wines it stocks and allows a customer to search through its list of wines according to region or price. Once the customer has found the wine he wants, he can place an order over the Internet. The wine-merchant could then send an electronic mail back to the customer saying that his wine has been placed on his behalf in their bonded cellar or could ship it via courier to the customer.

● Buying a car over the Internet might not seem to be a natural choice, but the car makers have gone to considerable lengths to provide customers with as much information as possible. Customers can sign up for incentive award schemes, can download a screen-saver utility with pictures of the cars or, in the case of one car manufacturer, view the current traffic conditions courtesy of the car maker.

● Stockbrokers on the Internet are growing in number and provide a crossover between real and electronic products. Once the customer has filled in an electronic form online giving bank details and references, the stockbroker can assign the user a user name and secure password. From now on, the customer can easily monitor real-time share prices and instruct the stockbroker to buy or sell shares. The confirmation of the transaction would be sent by electronic mail back to the customer. The added advantage is that the portfolio pricing could be imported into the customer's spreadsheet or accounts package.

How to transfer files

There are several ways of getting a file to your customer. You could send the file from your electronic mail software or you could store it on an Internet server and allow users to download it using special software.

Delivering online real-time information

Sending files by electronic mail

Almost all electronic mail packages allow you to attach a file to a message. For example, if you want to send a spreadsheet to a colleague, you could send her an electronic mail message saying 'enclosed are the figures for this month' and attach the spreadsheet file to the message. The electronic mail package will then encode the file and send it as normal to the recipient. When she receives the message, her mail package will decode the file and she will see that there is a file attached to the message which she can open with her spreadsheet software such as Excel or 1-2-3.

The process of encoding the file is important, since it ensures that the file is transferred correctly. There is one big problem with sending messages that are not text over the Internet – the Internet was really only designed to handle text and files often contain data or are programs. This means that you need to encode the file to fool the

Internet into thinking that it's handling text. There are two ways of encoding your files to convert them into a pseudo-text form that can be carried over all Internet links. The first encoding method is called UUencode and the second is called MIME.

Downloading files

When you move around the World Wide Web, viewing pages and clicking on hyperlinks, you are browsing; many Web pages also have links that lead to a file rather than to another Web page – if you click on one of these download links, your Web browser will automatically start to download the file on to your hard disk.

The Internet is exciting because there is such a wide range of different types of software that you can download and use at home. For example, many of the large software companies, such as Microsoft and Lotus, have trial versions of new or popular software that you can download and use before deciding whether to buy the full program. Some Web sites are dedicated to provide a store of files that you can download. Look at 'www.shareware.com' or 'www.download.com' and you will find thousands of files.

There are demonstration versions of games that work for a few days or have a limited number of levels. The new Internet technologies normally require new software, and this is often available free to download – for example, the PointCast news broadcasting system. If you want to view video or listen to audio over the Internet, you will need to add a special module to your Web browser to allow it to support this feature. These modules – called plug-ins – are made available as the new techniques are developed and can be downloaded free to keep your Web browser up to date. The Internet also allows you to download the latest drivers for graphics hardware and modems; if you have a problem with an application, download a special program that fixes the fault – called a patch.

If you are interested in new software, there are millions of different shareware programs that you can download. If you like the program and use it regularly, you pay a registration fee to the developer. Shareware programs cover the whole range of applications and include diaries, drawing and painting programs, word processor and writing programs, business tools and much more.

If you want to add new fonts to your system or enhance a presentation with exciting graphic images, look on the Internet. There are thousands of different fonts created by professional designers – some are available to download free, others can be tried out for free. The Internet started as a way of sharing information and on it there are hundreds of millions of files that contain useful information covering just about every subject. If you want to find the telephone number of a local plumber or the population statistics of a country, the Internet will have information files that can be viewed, downloaded and printed.

The main drawback in downloading information is that the bigger the file, the longer it will take to transfer over your modem link to your computer. For example, a full trial version of a Microsoft product such as Frontpage is stored in a file that is over 20Mb in size. Even with a high-speed modem, this would take most of a day to transfer to your computer! In some countries, local telephone calls are free so this is not a problem, but in the UK you will have to pay for the trial software in the cost of your telephone bill.

Download time

There are many different factors that affect the time it will take to transfer a file to your computer. If you had a direct telephone link to the remote computer, then it would be easy to work out the time it would take and you would know that the time taken would come down if you used a faster modem.

Unfortunately, the Internet has its own delays; if there are a lot of other users also trying to download the same file as you, then this will cause delays. If the file is stored on a slow computer, it will slow down the process and, lastly, if the file is stored on a computer in another country, then you are relying on the speed of the links between your ISP and the other country.

You will find that, on average, a 1Mb file will take around 10–20 minutes to download if you have a fast modem (7–15 minutes if you have the newest high-speed modem). Sometimes, you will pick a file stored on a high-speed computer at a quiet moment on the Internet and it will fly across.

One of the worries for many users is the threat of virus attacks. Most of the big, well-known Web sites are regularly scanned against viruses and the software that you can download is also scanned. However, there is a chance of picking up a virus if you download files – see the next few pages for more information on how to protect your computer.

Tip

As you use the Internet, you might think that it slows down sometimes – you are quite right! As more users connect to the Internet, there is more information being transferred and the links cannot always cope with the amount of information. This is most noticeable in the early afternoon when people in the USA wake up and start to connect. From 2 p.m. onwards, the Internet slows down considerably and any file download will take much longer. The worst time to use the Internet is in the late afternoon: users in the USA are connected and people in the UK are getting home after work and playing with the Internet. The best time is mid-morning – in the early morning office computers are connected as users check their mail messages. Don't forget, though, that the mid-morning is also the most expensive time for telephone calls. The cheapest time is over the weekend.

How to download

There's really only one way to transfer a file from your computer to a server (uploading) or from the server back to your computer (downloading) and this is by using a set of commands called FTP – file transfer protocol. FTP describes a way of encoding file data and sending it in chunks from one computer to another. You don't have to know how FTP works nor care too much, since it's as complicated as copying a file from your hard disk to a floppy disk!

There are generally two ways of FTPing a file (FTP has been turned into a verb as well as a noun by Internet folk); either use a special FTP software utility or use your WWW browser to do the same job. I'll show you both ways, since you will need to use a special FTP program to upload files to your server (which is useful when storing Web pages or other files on the server), but your customers can easily download files just using a WWW browser.

The first thing to do if you want to download a file using FTP is to find an Internet server that has been set up to allow FTP file transfers. It's important to note that unless you specifically instruct the server to allow any user the access to download a file, they won't be allowed to. I'm going to use the Microsoft Internet site as an example, because it will always have some files you can download using FTP. Here are the steps you need to take to download a copy of the Microsoft Internet Explorer WWW browser program.

Steps using a browser

1. Enter the name of the FTP server in the URL address field. In this case, we want to look at the files we can download from Microsoft, so we enter 'ftp://www.microsoft.com'. Notice that instead of starting the address with 'http' (for a Web page), we're using 'ftp' to tell the browser we want to look at files.

2. Your browser will display a list of the folders and files you can look at. It's rather similar to using the Windows Explorer or Program Manager under Windows to see the files stored on your hard disk. The difference is that these files are stored on Microsoft's computer in Seattle.

3. Move your mouse pointer to the folder called 'IE' and click once to open the folder.

4. Move your mouse pointer over the file called 'IE.EXE' and double-click on the program.

5. Your browser will now automatically sense that you want to download this file and will pop up a window asking where to store the file. It will then start to transfer the file (which could take up to an hour).

Steps using FTP software

1. Enter the name of the FTP server you want to contact and enter the name and password. Almost all Internet servers that allow you to transfer files provide for guests (that's you) using something called anonymous login. This means you use the user name 'anonymous' and enter your e-mail address as the password (nothing will happen against you, and it's polite to do this to help the computer supervisor at the other end work out who's using his files).

2. Press the connect button and the FTP software will try and connect to the distant server – in this case Microsoft's computer.

3. Once you are connected, you'll see a list of folders and files – just as in the browser example above.

4. Move your mouse pointer over the folder called 'IE' and click to open and view its contents.

5. Move your mouse pointer over the file called 'IE.EXE' and double-click on the line.

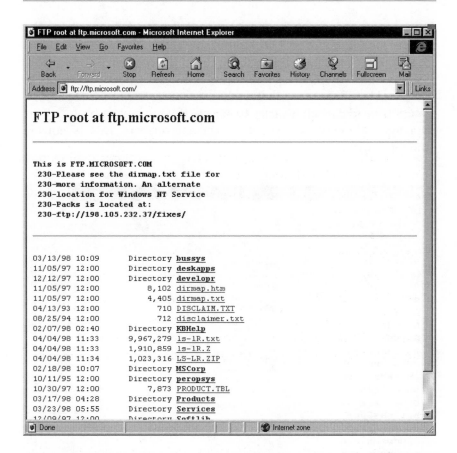

FTP using a Web browser

6. The FTP software will now download this file into the directory on your hard disk that's indicated on the left of the screen.

Securing files on the Internet

In this chapter I have explained how easy it is for a user to download a file from your Internet site. This does not mean that any files stored on your Internet site will be readily available to anyone who cares to download the data. There would be no point in placing your company's intellectual property or publications in a public place.

When you set up your Internet site (see Chapter 10) you will generally protect the files from being downloaded by any user. Most

Internet servers can be easily set up so that potential customers can browse your WWW pages but cannot download file using FTP unless they have specific permission to do so.

The whole question of security of files and data is discussed in Chapter 11. Suffice to say that if you do want customers to be able to access your files, then it's easy to set up. If you want to protect your data against everyone except choice subscribers, this is equally straightforward.

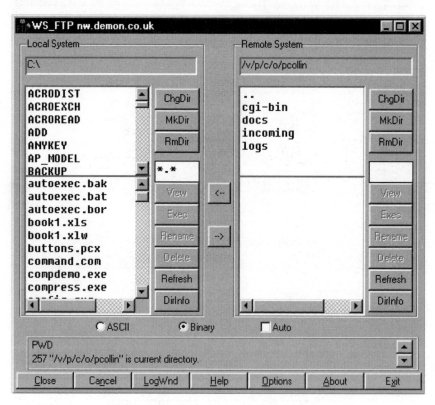

FTP with a dedicated application

Providing data on the Internet

The best way to provide value added benefit to the visitors of your Web site is to include data. You might simply include a list of forthcoming conferences, relevant books or product specifications, or you might want to link your company's office database directly to the Web.

There is a great potential for companies to get the most from the Internet by becoming information providers. Rather than running a simple passive Web site or one that you update manually, why not allow your visitors to search for information?

Online publishing of a database

Two excellent examples of companies that provide great Web sites are the AutoTrader car sales newspaper and the AA hotel guides. The AutoTrader system links its main advertisements database directly to the its Web site – a visitor to its Web site can search for a particular car make or model and see the current adverts. What you see is exactly what is in the database as new advertisers telephone AutoTrader!

The AA presents just as much information on its Web site, but does not provide such fast updates to the data. Its Web site lets a visitor search a database of all the hotels in the UK and displays a photograph, description text and contact details.

How it works

Both these examples use an Internet server that's based in the company. The process of creating a link to a database program is as follows:

1. The Internet server is linked to the a database program that manages the data files.

2. When a user visits the Web site and types in a search question, this query is passed to the Internet server.

3. The Internet server passes the query to the database program.

4. The database program searches for the data and formats the answers.

5. The formatted answer text is sent back to the visitor.

In order to set up a system that links your company's data to your Web site allowing a visitor to search the information you will need a reasonably complex system. You really need your own in-house Internet server with a server program and a link to the Internet (this can be by ISDN or, ideally, leased line). You will also need a database application that will run on your Internet server or a link to another server which is running the database application. Lastly, you need to set up a form on your Web site to accept a visitor's query and a script that will pass the query to the database application.

Setting up a database link to the Internet is very rewarding, both for your company's profile and for the users on the Internet. However, it does require a considerable amount of time, effort and money to employ a programmer to write the scripts and connect the database to the Internet server.

Integrated database and Web design software

Many of the new breed of Web page design software include functions to simplify the process of publishing a database on your Web site. Each program has a different method of tackling the problem and each has its own merits. For example, Microsoft's FrontPage Web design software allows you to add an Access database to your Web site to allow visitors to search the data. This is very easy to use and set up, but you do need to have an account with an ISP that supports this database extension; most ISPs that advertise support for FrontPage extensions do not support the database extensions.

Alternative products include Allaire's Coldfusion Web design software. This powerful suites of programs allows a team of developers and designers to produce complex database-driven Web sites. However, this program is not for a complete beginner – it's relatively expensive and complex to learn. In addition, you need to work with your ISP to ensure that they have the range of extensions on their server that ColdFusion requires.

Data publishing on a budget

If the previous section puts you off the idea of publishing data on to the Internet, then there are simpler ways of allowing a visitor to search for information. The drawback is that you cannot use your existing database program (which might run under Microsoft Windows); instead, you will need to use the Perl programming language to create scripts (called CGI scripts) that run on the Internet server.

If you are using an ISP to host your Web site, then this solution is really the only option you have to allow visitors to search for information on your site.

The system works as follows: save your data either in separate files for each item (useful if you have just a few dozen items with lots of text) or save your data as separate lines in a few large files (which is useful if you have lots of small items of text). For example, if you want to provide a database of twenty forthcoming conventions together with a description and dates, you might put the details of each convention into a different file. However, if you have a simple dictionary or glossary, you might store each word and definition on a separate line of a single large file.

These data files (which would normally be just plain text files or HTML-formatted files) are stored in a separate folder with your main Web site page files on your ISP's computer – you transfer the files on to the remote computer using FTP.

To let a visitor search any of these data files you will need two more items: a Web page with a form that lets the user enter a search term and a script that will actually search through each word in each file to find a match.

How it works

1. The visitor enters a search word in the form displayed on a Web page.

2. The Web page calls a small program called a script that runs on the ISP's computer.

3. The script searches through the data files and pulls out the lines of text that contain the search word.

4. The script formats the lines and sends them back to the visitor.

As you can appreciate, the central feature of this system is the script that searches the files and formats the results.

To write a script that can carry out these functions is not easy. You should either contact your ISP, who might already have a library of scripts written ready for you to use, or you will need to hire a programmer to do the work for you. The programming language that is most often used to write scripts is called Perl and the system of connecting your Web page to the script is called CGI. If you search the Web (using 'www.yahoo.com') for CGI tutorials you will get a good grounding in the language.

Publishing documents on the Internet

In the previous sections I have given an outline of the way you might go about providing a database that can be searched by visitors to your Web site. Rather than letting visitors search through a database, you might want to publish a text – such as a monthly journal or company report – directly on the Internet.

You could create a Web page that contains all the text of the document, limiting access to this Web page using password access (see Chapter 9 for more details on access security). An alternative is to store a document file on the Web server and allow users to download the document file to read on their word processor or using a view such as Adobe Acrobat.

If you want to publish a document text on to the Internet you will need to create the file and save it to the ISP's computer where you store your Web pages. You would then either include a link to the file within a Web page – allowing visitors to download the file using FTP – or your could password protect the file and ask for payment and registration.

For example, if you have a Web site on your ISP's computer under

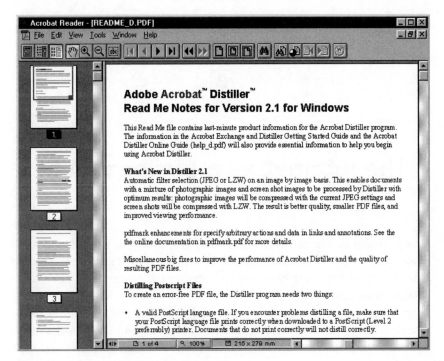

Publishing with Adobe Acrobat

the domain name 'simon.co.uk' that holds all your Web page documents in a folder called '/docs', then you could create a sub-directory
folder under this to hold your document files, calling it '/publish'. The
document file, called 'journal1.doc' would be stored in the '/publish'
folder and the complete path to the file would be 'simon.co.uk/
docs/publish/journal1.doc'.

To let visitors download this document file from your Web site, you
could add a hotlink to the file within one of your Web pages. The
HTML code for the link would be: '

```
Click <A HREF = 'ftp://journal 1.doc'> here
</A> to download the first part of this
month's Journal.
```

If you want to charge visitors for the privilege of downloading the
document, you would protect the '/publish' directory and place this
link in a protected Web page that requires a user name and password
– see Chapter 9 for more details.

8

The Internet as a Business Tool

The Internet is a great sales and marketing tool that provides a new way of reaching potential customers, but it's also extremely important as a tool that can help improve communications and cut costs within your company.

The Internet is a worldwide network that lets any registered user connect using basic tools: you need a computer, a modem and a telephone link. Once you have this connection you can send information to any other user on the Internet. This information could be e-mail messages, spreadsheet files, video clips or audio.

In this chapter, I'll show you the potential of the Internet as a business tool. It lets you keep in touch with distant sales teams, travelling employees or other companies. Keeping in touch doesn't just mean sending text messages. The Internet lets you send video or audio data from one user to another; using this you can now create a video conferencing system that links two or more Internet users. Video and sound is transferred live. A simpler application is to use the Internet as a replacement for your telephone calls – each user has a microphone and speakers connected to their computer and the sound is transmitted over the Internet. Best of all, the video or sound is transmitted for free or, at most, the price of a local call – no more long-distance phone bills!

Telephone over the Internet

One recent scheme is to use the Internet as a replacement for your normal telephone provider. Think about it: your time on the Internet only costs you the price of a local call and yet you can transmit information to any other location in the world. All you need is to transmit sound in real time and you have a very cheap alternative to the telephone. (It's no wonder that telephone companies are getting worried.)

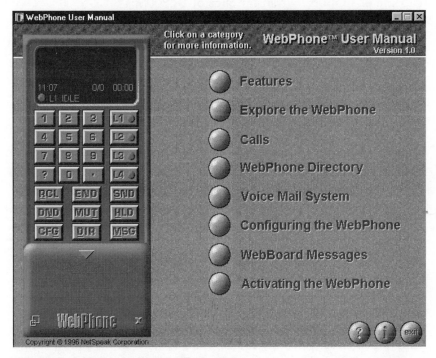

Cheap international calls using the Web

To set up a telephone system that uses the Internet you need to equip your computer with some extra hardware and run a special software program. You will need to add a sound card, speakers and a microphone to your computer (although some multimedia computers already have these fitted). The sound card converts sound from the microphone into a numeric form that can be handled by the computer and does the reverse when feeding sound to the speakers. Don't forget that the people at each end of the telephone needs these extras.

To manage the link and transfer the sound data over the Internet you need to install an extra program that will manage the flow of data and try and prevents breaks in the sound. Newer versions of Web browsers (such as Netscape Navigator 3) now include the features to support these telephone features, but otherwise you will need to buy an application such as NetPhone.

The software lets you 'connect' to another user on the Internet and will compress your voice and transmit it to the other user. In order to get reasonable sound quality, you need a fast modem – at least one capable of supporting transfer rates of 28,800bps.

Once installed and running, the software is very easy to use. Both of you need to be connected to the Internet at the same time, but otherwise there are few problems. You can talk to any other user anywhere in the world for the price of a local call!

Video conferencing on the Internet

A development of the telephone system described above is to transmit both live sound and video signals over the Internet. This lets you carry out a video conference with several other people on the Internet, without any expensive satellite links or studio time.

In order to set up your computer ready for video conferencing over the Internet, you will need to buy extra hardware for your computer and install some control software. The quality of the sound and the video will depend on the speed of your link to the Internet – the faster the better. Ideally, you should have an ISDN link, but a very fast modem will just about manage to carry still pictures and sound.

To configure your computer you will need to add a video camera (tiny personal cameras are available for around £150) plus a sound card with microphone and speakers. You will also need to install video conferencing software and have a fast link to the Internet.

Once configured, you can connect to any other user (such as another office) and transfer video images. If you have a slow modem connection to the Internet you'll only see the video pictures updated every minute. If you have a fast ISDN connection you can see a rather jerky video with new pictures every few seconds.

Electronic mail for distribution

Electronic mail is covered in depth in Chapter 3, but do not forget that you can use it to send any type of data – not just text messages. You can use your e-mail software to send documents to the members of your sales force: picture files of new products, sales reports or pricing charts.

Electronic mail is a great way to keep in touch with customers –

sending them updates to manuals, new material on a product or even a demonstration program to try out.

Keeping in touch with distant employees

The Internet is a perfect business tool to keep in touch with a network of offices or employees. Many companies are now starting to link their internal company networks in different buildings or countries via the Internet. After all, why go to the expense of buying and setting up ISDN links or leased lines between two company sites when you can use the Internet to do the same job, and have all its other benefits too?

A more modest use of the Internet would be for travelling employees or those working at home to use it to keep in touch with the office. You can send mail to any user and send your colleagues files or documents to work on.

Here are a number of ways in which you could use the Internet to cut costs and improve communications with distant colleagues.

● Keep homeworkers informed with what's going on in the office, using e-mail.

● Send travelling sales reps picture files of new products or sales reports.

● Use automated e-mail (see Chapter 3) to send reps and customers information in reply to their questions (such as new price-lists or distributor information).

● Set up an online database for your customers and sales team to check availability of a product in your warehouse with a live data link (see Chapter 7).

● Set up a private Web page or mailing list for colleagues to send you sales tips, industry rumours or other company information.

● Create an online diary to allow distant colleagues to make appointments to come into the office.

● Use the Internet for long-distance telephone calls with colleagues.

● Set up video conferencing with another office on the other side of the world – at a local rate telephone call.

● Use the Internet as a way of linking two or more office networks.

Security on the Internet

This chapter covers security: a growing problem on the Internet in general and a particular headache for administrators who manage sites with sensitive or commercial information. Security on the Internet or an intranet is a worry because the Internet was originally developed as an 'open' system to share information between colleges and universities. Now that business wants to use it, it needs to have security added!

There are several problems to address when establishing security – some are for your benefit, others are for the benefit of the visitors to your site. For example, if a user visits a site, how does the user know that this really is run by the company who claims to run it? If I visit the site of a big company and purchase goods online, I want to be sure that this site really is that company's site before I hand over my credit card details.

From your point of view, you will want to address local security access. For example, how do I allow authorized users into areas of the server but prevent unauthorized or unregistered users from viewing other areas of the site? You will also want to make sure that hackers or others keen on wreaking havoc cannot gain access to your server, utilities or password files. In short, you want to prove that you are a secure sever to visitors and to ensure that you are a secure server against hackers.

The solutions

The first job you must do when creating a Web site is to ensure that the files have the correct security attributes. These file access attributes determine what a visitor to your site can do with each file. Wrong attribute settings are one of the main causes of basic security faults on new Web sites.

Once you have the file attributes defined, your main defence in the fight for privacy is encryption. This involves scrambling text and messages using an encryption algorithm and an encryption key. Only the intended recipient with the correct decryption key can unscramble the text and read the original message. This style of protection – encrypting the messages – is used in the main security standards that you will come across: SSL (secure sockets layer) and S/MIME (secure multipart Internet mail encoding). SSL is covered in Chapter 6, with regard to setting up a secure payment system online.

Protecting files on your Web site

Running a Web site poses many security problems that you have to do your best to minimize. If you have an account with an ISP and use their computer to store your Web pages, then you have less control over some security aspects than if you had your own Internet server in your company.

When you create a Web page, it is stored on a computer connected to the Internet. This computer could be in your office (if you have your own office Internet server) or it could be on a computer at an ISP. You have to log on to the computer before it will allow you to carry out commands. If you have an ISP account, then you would dial up the ISP with your modem; if you have an internal Internet server you would connect via your network.

Once connected, the server software will ask you for a user name and password. It checks these two pieces of information against its database of names. If they are correct, it will allow you to access your part of the server's hard disk on which your Web pages are stored. If either the name or password are wrong, you will not get full access to all the files.

Now that you have access to the server, you will normally see several directories that contain different data files. One directory will contain the files that make up your public Web pages that can be accessed by anyone. The other directories are private and will not be visible to any other user except the authorized administrator. These other directories might contain data files that are searched by your Web pages, usage logs and so on.

Special attributes attached to each file and directory tell the server software whether it can allow a user access. The administrator is the only person who can change these attributes and so change the basic security of a server. For example, you can set up a very insecure server in which every directory and all the files that are stored on the server can be read by any user. The attributes also allow the administrator to define if a file can be executed (run) by a user, read, modified or deleted – so you have a lot of control over what the public can see on your server.

A lot of Internet servers run the Unix operating system; the Internet server software runs on top of this. There are also versions of the server software that will run on Microsoft Windows. If you are using an Internet server that runs Unix, or if you connect to an ISP using Unix (most do; if in doubt – ask them) you will need to learn a few commands that will set up the security levels of files and directories.

The first time that you store a new Web page file on a server, it is normally assigned default attributes that prevent anyone reading it – except the administrator. To allow any user to view the HTML file for a Web page, you need to change its attributes to read access. To do this under Unix, you'll need to enter the command 'chmod 604 filename.html'. If you want to prevent all users from reading a file, enter the command 'chmod 0 filename.html'. These commands vary depending on the server, so check first.

A secure Web site

Creating a secure Web site usually means adding the SSL (secure sockets layer) protocol to the Web server. A Web server normally sends information to and from the user's computer over the public open Internet – allowing anyone with access the opportunity to view the information. If you set up a secure Web server, this information is scrambled before being transmitted over the Internet.

If you want to set up a Web site allowing visitors the chance to buy goods online – for example with a credit card – then you will need to provide a secure environment to assure the safety of the visitor's card details. The usual way of creating this secure environment is to set up SSL security. This standard is included in just about every commercial Web server product that is aimed at online business users. It has the great advantage in that it is also directly supported by the Netscape and Microsoft IE Web browsers (the status of the session is indicated by the key icon in the lower left corner of the screen: a broken key is a connection to an un-secure server, a full key shows a session to a secure SSL server).

For further information on SSL and the other security systems used to provide an environment to allow visitors to buy online, see Chapter 6.

Secure electronic mail

In a standard installation, any user sending a mail message to another user on the Internet or intranet is sending a plain text copy of the message that any hacker could intercept and read with little difficulty. The same applies for attachments that are sent in their plain file format without encryption.

Even – or perhaps more so – within a company intranet, mail messages will contain sensitive information and so the sender would much rather keep this information private. There are three main techniques to secure your electronic mail transfers:

1. Encrypt the mail message body (not the header with destination) and any attachment using a third-party encryption scheme such as PGP (see Chapter 6 for more details on PGP). The recipient will need to run the message through the decryption tool to read the original message.

2. Use a secure mail client that implements encryption and authentication technology such as S/MIME. This is a good standard for e-mail transfers but does require an authenticated certificate.

3. Use a secure mail server.

Managing access to your Web site

Once you have set up your Web site you might want to prevent users from accessing certain pages until they have applied for authorization. For example, you might want to put up sales data for your sales representatives that you don't want anyone else to see. You might also want to publish a journal or newsletter onto the Web which you want to prevent users reading until they pay for the privilege. Lastly, you might want to monitor closely the type of customer that reads your pages, and so you would want to set up a security system that asks the user to complete a registration form before they can access the Web site.

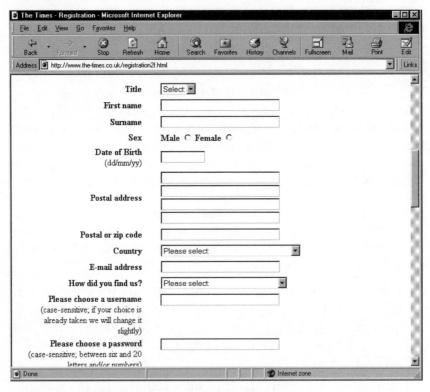

Registration form before site access is granted

All of these scenarios make use of a password authorization feature that's available with most ISPs and with an internal company Internet server. It works as follows: you place the Web pages that you want to protect into a special directory on the Web server. In this directory you create a user-password file; each time a user tries to access a Web page that is stored in this directory, the Web server software will spot the user-password file and will pop up a dialog box asking the user to enter a user name and password. The software then checks this against the file and allows access if there is a correct match.

To set up this type of security is very straightforward, but will vary depending on the type of Web server software you or your ISP are using. One way of creating a protected site would be to follow these steps:

1. Create a Web home page which asks the user if she has registered.

2. If the user has not registered, a Web page with a registration form is displayed.

3. This form is submitted to an authentication program that generates a unique user name and password for this user. These are also automatically stored in the user-password file.

4. If the user has registered, then she can view the 'secret' Web pages in the protected directory.

5. The action of calling up a page in the protected directory will automatically prompt the user to enter her name and password. If these are correct, she can view the page.

Choosing a password

The manager of your Web site – the person that has permission to copy files and change the contents of any page – has a unique user name and a password. It is worth going to some trouble to come up with a password that will be very difficult for a hacker to guess. The most secure type of password is a combination of letters and numbers with both upper and lower case. For example, you dog's name is not a secure password. But change the case of a couple of the letters and replace a letter with a number and it becomes almost impossible to guess at.

Firewalls

Once everyone started to talk about the Internet and its security problems, consultants and security companies advised that the only way to protect your company against hackers was to use a firewall. Unfortunately, few people understood what a firewall was or what it did.

The first point to make is that there's no need to install a firewall unless you have a direct link between the Internet and your office network. For example, if you have installed an Internet server in your office and have connected it to your company network, then you need a firewall. If, however, you dial into the Internet on an occasional basis to check for electronic mail or to maintain a Web site stored on an ISP's server, then you don't need a firewall.

A firewall is a special software application that looks at all the raw data that's transferred to and from the Internet. You can configure the firewall software to look for particular types of data, for example commands that should not be run on your Internet server. You could also configure the firewall to block any data that originates from a particular user or country.

When a user – either friendly or malicious – tries to access your Internet server, they send commands to the server to ask it to carry out actions. If a user wants to view a Web page, the WWW browser sends commands to the server asking it to send back the data for a particular page, which it can then display. Normally, a user doesn't see this transfer of data, and if your Internet server is only accessed by friendly visitors, there would be no need for a firewall.

A hacker will try and see what other data files you have stored on your Internet server – not just the Web pages you want to show the public. If you have a link between the Internet server and your office network then a hacker would try and fool the Internet server into allowing him to access your main office server and all the sensitive data it contains.

The job of the firewall is to block these unauthorized commands but allow through unhindered any genuine commands. A good firewall should not get in the way of a friendly visitor, but should totally block the actions of a hacker. This is, as you can imagine, a difficult area since hackers are always finding ways around new techniques.

Many new server software products, such as Microsoft's IIS and Netscape's server software, include features that let you configure your server to block a wide range of techniques used to break in to servers. Make sure that you take time to learn how to configure the software and make sure that you do set up the security levels to block unauthorized commands.

The technology is changing so often that you would be best advised to look at the experience of other users. Look at newsgroups on the Internet that cover firewalls – such as 'comp.security' – and search for vendors that supply firewall software by searching a database like Yahoo! (at 'www.yahoo.com').

Types of firewall

There are, generally, two types of firewall available. The simplest tool is called a packet filter and looks at each bit of the raw data coming in from the Internet. (The raw data sent over the Internet is organized into packets for convenience during transmission. Each packet has a destination and source address, but these can be changed by a clever hacker to fool firewalls.)

To configure a packet filter, you edit a filter table that contains various rules that will block or allow each packet as it is examined. For example, you could define a rule that packets from a particular address should be blocked – which would stop most hackers. However, it's relatively simple to change the source address of a packet, which would get around this filter. Alternatively, you could define a rule that prevents data going to a particular part of the server or similar rules. Once you have set up your table, it is transferred to the router (the communications device) that links your Internet server to the ISP's Internet point – this could be an ISDN device or a device used on a leased line.

The second type of firewall is called a bastion host. This is a very basic dedicated computer that sits between the link to the Internet and your Internet server. It contains the absolute minimum number of data files required and spends its time checking data and, if it passes, sending it to the Internet server to be processed. Using a bastion host means your office will have three dedicated computers: the office server, the Internet server and the bastion host.

Neither of these techniques is foolproof and there are ways of improving security further. For example, some clever hackers can skip past all these security arrangements and configure the data they send to look like data from a user on your network. To get around this problem you would need to fit network monitoring tools that can spot rogue data.

Virus attacks

A virus attack can be very damaging to any computer, and especially to a company network that links many computers together. A virus is a vicious little program that attaches itself to another program and copies itself to any hard disk available. After a period of time, it might delete your files, corrupt your data or simply display a harmless message. Whichever type of virus it is, you want to stop it getting into your system.

What is a virus?

A virus is a nasty little software program that buries itself within another program. It will then emerge and try to damage your data or delete your files. The big problem with a virus is that if you copy a file it will try and copy itself at the same time, so it can soon infect all your disks and any other computers. The programmers who create a new virus try to make it as destructive as possible and hard to find. The main way that you can catch a virus is by downloading unchecked software from the Internet.

How you catch a virus

There are two ways a virus could enter your system from the Internet (there are plenty of ways it can get a virus without the Internet!). The first is from a file that has been downloaded from a remote computer and the second is within an electronic mail message.

In order to prevent an infected file being downloaded, you have to be very strict with the types of Internet programs that can be used in your business. For example, to prevent users downloading a file, you could stop them from using the FTP program. Unfortunately, this does not stop users with a Web browser from downloading a file: many Web pages have a hot spot that says 'click me to download a demonstration program' or similar. In this case, it's very difficult to prevent the Web browser downloading the file.

For most users, it's better to explain the potential problems and to equip each computer with an anti-virus kit. If a user really must download a demonstration program or another file, then the FTP program or the Web browser that's used for the download should be set up to store the file in one directory. Once it has been downloaded – and before it is opened or run – it should be checked with a virus detection utility. There are good virus checkers by McAfee and Dr Soloman. Once the file is checked, you can open the document or run the program.

There are extra problems with files that have been compressed. It's common to 'zip' a file (to compress it) so that it takes less time to download. In this case, it's very difficult for virus checkers to spot a compressed virus – but some can. In these cases, unzip (decompress) the compressed file to a floppy disk or into a separate directory and immediately check your entire hard disk for virus infection.

These measures might sound rather cumbersome and time-consuming. It is actually very unusual to catch a virus when download-ing files, but just imagine how your business would operate if you did get infected and all your data became corrupted. Is it worth the risk?

The second way a virus could enter your system is through an elec-tronic mail message. This is a relatively new experience that is very rare – but still worth checking. In Chapter 7, I showed you how easy it is to send files and other data via a mail message over the Internet. Data is normally included with your mail message as an attachment. Until you open the attachment, you only have the sender's word that it contains the file he mentions. However, it's a good way for a virus to spread unnoticed.

In order to spot a mail message or attachment that is infected, you need to install special software that can scan mail messages and their attachments as they arrive at your Internet server. There are a num-ber of products available that work with different types of mail sys-tems and operating systems – your Internet provider should be able to help you choose suitable software.

Anti-virus software

There are dozens of virus detection software available, and many are available to try out before you buy. You can even download a trial pro-gram from the Internet and use this for (typically) 30 days before you will have to pay for the program. For example, the popular VirusScan software from Symantec is just one of many trial versions of virus detection programs that you can download. Once you have down-loaded and installed the software, it can be used for 30 days before it stops working. Thirty days is plenty of time to use the software and see if you like it. If you do like it and want to continue using it, you will need to buy the full program. To download the trial software, visit the 'www.symantec.com' Web site for full instructions.

If your computer already has a virus detection software program supplied as part of a package, then make sure that you run the soft-ware each time you download new files from the Internet.

Plug-in or applet attacks

I have called this section 'applet attacks' because it concerns a new risk that's not really been classified as a virus or as a hacker. Once you start reading the computer press you will soon hear of two relatively

new technologies: Java and ActiveX. Both these are types of programming language used to create little programs – called applets –
that carry out some function in a complex Web page.

Plug-ins and applets are special pieces of software that extend the
functions of a Web browser. If a new way of displaying video over the
Internet is developed, you will need to install a plug-in that allows
your Web browser to display the video images. Plug-ins are normally
required for new multimedia features in Web sites, such as video,
audio, three-dimensional graphics and animation; luckily, plug-ins are
supplied free and install themselves automatically.

The developer creating a Web page can add extra functions that
are not normally available by writing a little Java or ActiveX applet.
Once he has done this – it might move an icon around the screen or
create a ticker-tape message at the bottom of the screen – he includes
it in his Web page. New versions of Web browsers are compatible
with both Java and ActiveX and will automatically download the
applet and run it.

The idea behind both technologies is that they allow a competent
developer to create eye-catching Web pages without the user realiz-
ing he has downloaded a tiny 'helper' program. As you can imagine,
these are an ideal way of wreaking havoc on your computer if used
by a hacker. You might have every virus checker possible installed,
but when you visit the wrong Web page, your browser would automatically download a rogue applet which could, potentially, delete
your files.

To counter this, the makers of Java and ActiveX – Sun and
Microsoft respectively – have built in features to prevent their development tools being used by hackers. You can also configure your
browser to ignore these applets. For more information on the potential threat and how to protect yourself, visit the 'www.microsoft.com'
site for ActiveX and 'www.sun.com' for Java.

Safe use of plug-ins

Security is always important, and especially so when you are downloading a plug-in from a (possibly) unknown supplier to carry out an
uncertain function on a Web page. To help spot these potential risks,
both popular brands of Web browser – from Microsoft and Netscape
– will warn you that you are about to transfer a plug-in or send personal information over an open link. Sometimes, this warning is not
necessary – if you typed in a search word to find a Web site using a

search engine then you know that you have typed in the information and there is no problem. In other situations, you might have forgotten that the information that you are sending could be intercepted by a hacker.

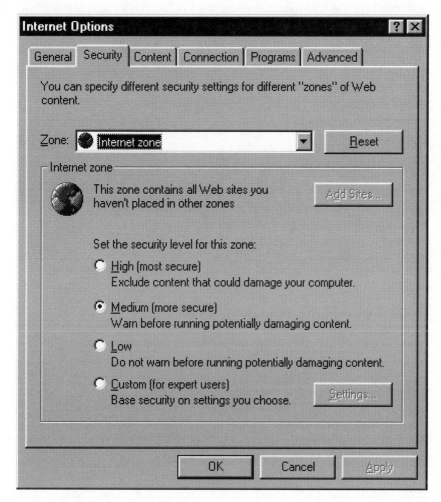

Security options on your Web browser

Whenever you type information into a Web page and click a button, your Web browser will display a warning box to alert you that you could be sending confidential information. When you see this warning box, make sure that you are not sending your credit card information or other confidential text and then click on the 'OK' button.

If you are visiting a special secure Web site that provides online shopping, your Web browser will detect this and tell you that you are now entering a safe environment. Anything that is sent to you or that you send back will be specially encrypted to prevent any hacker from reading the text. You can even send your credit card information in a safe and secure manner. You can configure the level of warning that the browser detects in IE using the 'View/Options/Security' screen and in Netscape using the 'Options/Security Preferences' screen.

10

Setting up a WWW Site

A WWW site is the most visible face of a company on the Internet. It acts as a shop front or catalogue that shows potential and existing customers your product range. You can provide a simple catalogue approach, using your WWW site simply to display text and pictures of your company and products, or you can create a more complex site that lets visitors search for information stored on your WWW site. Lastly, you can set up an advanced site that allows customers to order products, pay for them and (for some software products) take delivery of their purchase from your WWW site.

Your WWW site (which is also called a Web site or – incorrectly – a home page) is relatively straightforward to set up but requires time and planning: at least as much work as your general catalogue. After all, you are displaying your Web site in public to an audience of over 35 million people. This chapter will show you how to design and assemble a good Web site. To simplify the job of creating an effective Web site, many companies hire a professional WWW programmer – I will cover this separately later in the chapter and give you pointers on how to work with a programmer to produce what you want.

Registering a domain name

One of the most important steps in creating a web presence is to give your site an effective name. This will be used by visitors to access the site and is called a domain name; for example, 'www.microsoft.com' is the domain name of the Microsoft Corporation.

To register your domain name, find a name that is easy to remember and representative of your company. You can ask your ISP to do the paperwork, or you can do it yourself at 'www.internic.net' – the governing body for domain names. (Note that CompuServe, AOL and other OSPs do not allow you to use a unique domain name.) To check if your domain name has already been allocated, use the search feature at 'www.internic.net'.

What is a Web site?

Your WWW site is actually a collection of separate pages (some companies have just a couple of pages, others have tens of thousands). These pages are stored as text files that contain special formatting codes that describe how the text looks when displayed. These codes are part of a simple formatting language called HTML (hypertext

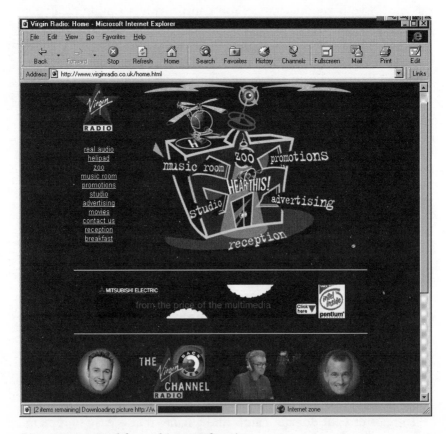

Live stereo sound from this complex site

markup language) that describes the size, colour and font of text together with any images, sound or video clips. Lastly, and most important, the HTML codes describe hypertext links that allow a user to navigate from one page to another.

The individual pages of a Web site are called Web pages and are normally stored in separate document files. Each Web page has a file name and is stored on the hard disk of the Internet server that hosts your domain. If this sounds confusing, it's simple: if you are using an OSP (such as CompuServe or AOL) to link to the Internet, your Web site will be a collection of Web pages (each in a separate file) stored on the OSP's computer system. If you are using an ISP (such as Pipex, Demon or Planet) you will store your Web pages on your section of their server's hard disk. Lastly, if you have decided to install your own Internet server in your company, then your Web pages will be stored on your own server's hard disk.

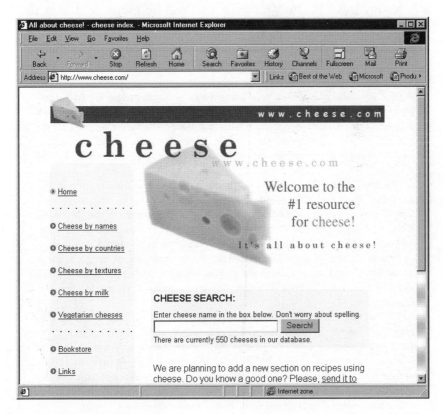

A clear, effective Web site

How do I view a Web site?

Once you have created a site and copied the individual files that make up your Web presence to the Internet server's hard disk, then it is possible for any other user on the Internet to view these pages. Any user that wants to look at Web sites (often called browsing or surfing the Web) will need to run software called a Web browser. There are several different types of browser available – including Netscape's Navigator and Microsoft's Internet Explorer. (See Chapter 2 for more information on Web browser software.)

Any user with a Web browser can now enter your URL (uniform resource locator) that uniquely identifies where on the Internet your Web pages are stored and view a page. Any formatted text that you included in the Web page will be sent to the user and displayed in exactly the same format you set up. If you included images (such as a company logo) in the Web page, this will be transferred over the Internet to the user and displayed on their screen.

How are Web pages accessed?

A user who wants to view a Web site enters the domain name for your company together with the filename for the individual Web page into their Web browser. The Web browser looks this up and then contacts the Internet server and asks for the correct Web page. Finally, the file that contains the Web page is sent back over the Internet and is decoded and displayed correctly by the browser.

The combination of your company's domain name and the filename of the individual Web page is called a URL. It normally looks something like 'http://www.microsoft.com/index.html'. The part on the far right of the URL is the filename that contains the Web page we want to look at – in this case it's called 'index.html'. The part on the far left tells the Web browser software that you want to look at a Web page and that it should talk to the distant server using a language called 'http'. Lastly, the section in the middle, 'www.microsoft.com' is the domain name of the company whose Web page we want to access – in this case, Microsoft Corporation.

The last piece of technical information regards the home page of a Web site. Each Web site has an initial contents page (normally called the home page). This gives you options of other Web pages that can be viewed on the site. This first home page is normally stored in a file called 'index.html'; because each site's home page is always stored in a file with the same name, you don't need to enter the full URL to access a site. For example, to view the home page of Microsoft Corp. you could either type in the URL 'http://www.microsoft.com/index.html' or simply 'http://www.microsoft.com'. Your Web browser will automatically ask for the 'index.html' file.

Who's looking at your Web site?

The Internet is very good at blinding users with numbers and statistics, but how can they be used for your business? There are over 35 million individuals who are connected to the Internet, which means you could have a vast potential audience.

Finding access log analysis tools – or ask your ISP

One of the key aspects to maintaining a good – and useful – Web site is to record visitor statistics. There are several ways of doing this, each of which provides more detailed information about the visitors. For practical examples showing how to record visitors, see later in this chapter.

The simplest way of checking the popularity of your Web site is to include a counter. These are currently all the rage on the WWW and say something like 'you are visitor 12345 to our site'. These normally work using a tiny program that runs on the Internet server and increments the counter each time a new user reads the file 'index.html' – your home page. They provide a simple way of checking how many users read your material.

To get feedback on the types of visitor to your Web site, you will need to record access logs for the Web pages. If you are using an ISP to host or store your Web pages, they will be able to provide daily or weekly logs. If you have your own server in-house, check the server software to see how it can produce access logs.

An entry into the access log is made each time a user reads a Web page. The information that is recorded is crucial and very useful for the marketing departments! It records the page that was read, the time and date it was read and the address of the visitor. You might now think that this provides a perfect way of getting a mailing list to e-mail these visitors with further information. Firstly, you would be almost banned from the Internet for sending unsolicited e-mails like this; secondly, the addresses are probably not correct. When an individual (not a company) connects to the Internet, they are given a unique address number; normally this address is different each time they log on. The only parts that are always the same are the country codes within the address.

To cut to the conclusion: you can use the access usage logs to find out which of your Web pages are most popular and in which country the visitors live.

The final way of finding out who is looking at your Web site is to ask the visitor to enter details about themselves. You can create an electronic questionnaire that is displayed as a separate Web page and asks the visitor to enter their name, areas of interest and perhaps a contact e-mail address. There's no guarantee that the information will be correct and you might have to offer a special offer to tempt visitors to complete the form.

Publicizing your Web site

Once you have designed and created your Web site and transferred it to the Internet server you are using, it's available to any passing visitor. Unfortunately, you are competing with tens of thousands of other Web sites, so you will need to do your utmost to make your site interesting and to publicize your site. I cover the subject of marketing on the Internet in Chapter 5, but this section concerns your Web site rather than your company profile.

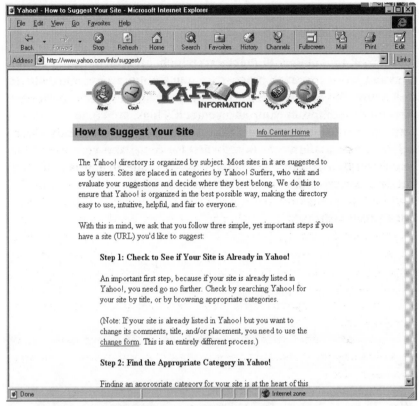

It's essential to be listed in search directories

Once you have a Web site, you must use it in just the same way as you would any other marketing resource. Make sure that the URL to your home page is on your business cards, products and stationery. This will generate a little traffic in visitors who come to have a look at your site. To publicize your Web site effectively, you need to ensure that your site's description and URL are easily available to any potential customer who might want to visit.

To try and bring order into the WWW, there are a number of directories – similar to a telephone directory – stored on the Web. These list hundreds of thousands of sites together with a short description and the URL at which you can reach the site. The real beauty of these online directories is that they can be searched.

If you want to find all the Web sites that have information regarding skyscrapers, you could search the directories for 'skyscrapers'. This particular enquiry will produce a list of several dozen Web sites which match this search. I have covered these directories in Chapter 4 from the opposite angle – that of a researcher – but it's just as important to make sure that your Web site is listed for others to see.

Each of the online directories (which are often called search engines) has a separate process for registering a new Web site. To make sure that your site is correctly registered, it's best to visit each directory and register your site yourself. There are some automated programs available that will send a summary of your Web site to between ten and two hundred directories to make sure that it's listed everywhere. Although very convenient, these automated registration tools can sometimes mis-register your site.

Using newsgroups

One of the most effective ways of publicizing your new Web site is to post a message to newsgroups. Newsgroups are discussion groups that cover over 40,000 individual topics, so there's bound to be at least one in your subject area.

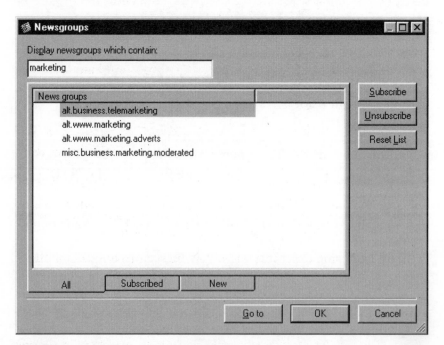

Publicizing carefully using newsgroups

If you publish dictionaries, you might find your best audience in an academic or teaching newsgroup together with a librarian's newsgroup. If the dictionary is on a specialist subject, try a newsgroup on this particular subject. When posting an advertisement like this, make very sure that it's brief and modest. If not, you will get flamed (sent rude messages) from the members of the newsgroup. You should also make quite sure that you do not duplicate your messages to too many similar newsgroups – this is called spamming and again will result in you being flamed.

Exchanging Web sites

The last job you should try and do to publicize your Web site is to try and swap URLs with other similar Web sites. If you produce dictionaries, try and get your dictionary Web site mentioned on a bookshop Web site; you can do the same in return.

Building a Web site

Making the decision to set up and maintain a Web site is not easy. It takes a considerable amount of time, money and effort to design, create and maintain a good, informative Web site. Before you start any of the design or construction of a site, you must first decide what you want your Web site to achieve for the company.

There are really just three possible basic purposes for any Web site, and these determine the money, effort and marketing required to set up and maintain the site.

1. **Corporate catalogue**. This is the simplest, least active of the possible Web sites. It provides a potential customer with your company and product details: it's really an electronic version of your corporate background or catalogue. There might also be lists of distributors or contacts where a customer might find your products. These sites are the simplest to set up, need little maintenance but are also the least exciting for the visitor.

2. **Marketing site**. This second type of Web site provides all the basic information about your company and its products and services, but also offers more to the visitor. There might be a simple search function that lets them look for particular information stored in archived material. You might have demonstration software or utilities available for download. Lastly, you might also have a simple

electronic questionnaire that lets visitors ask for more information. This type of site needs regular maintenance to keep the information up to date, and you will need to respond to any questions or queries sent by electronic mail. The site will take more effort to design, include links to other pages and perhaps to other sites that could be useful to the visitor.

3. **Interactive site**. This third type of Web site includes just about every Web design feature available! It allows a visitor to browse your product range and also offers secure methods for payment of goods. There might be a link to a company database that lets users query the database for information. The site would normally be based on an in-house Internet server and would need to be manned full-time to ensure that the database links are working, that any queries or electronic mail messages get a response and that customers purchasing goods receive their goods.

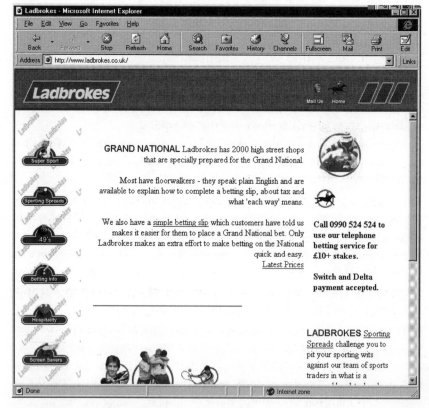

Marketing and interactive features combined

Once you have determined what you want your Web site to achieve, you can decide how much you should spend on the product. On the face of it, you could put up a Web site for just a few pounds per month, using an ISP to do all the hard work. However, this would be a simple site – and I have not counted the time to design or maintain the site. As a couple of extreme examples, there is a very impressive television news site based in the USA that looks great. It offers real-time news and weather with impressive design – but cost over \$10 million to implement. To counter this, there are plenty of small businesses that have set up simple sites that offer basic functions to customers. If you create and manage the site in your own time, you could easily create a good, useful site for around £600 per year.

Web page production

Each Web page on your site is made up of a several files:

● an HTML file that contains text, links to other pages and HTML formatting codes;

● graphic files that contains images, background patterns, icons or photographs – stored in GIF graphic file format (or the JPEG file format);

● data files to provide a searchable data source;

● sound files to provide sound for your Web pages;

● scripts that let you add functions to your Web pages.

The only file you really need is a file that contains HTML codes. These are full of the text you want to display together with HTML commands that describe the way the text should be formatted.

Creating HTML files

There are many ways to generate an HTML file. An HTML file is simply a plain text file that contains text and formatting codes – you can use complex Web page design tools to generate the files or you can type in the codes using a word processor. If you use one of the newer suites of software, such as Microsoft Office, then you can format a document in Word and choose 'Save As/HTML' to export the document to an HTML format file.

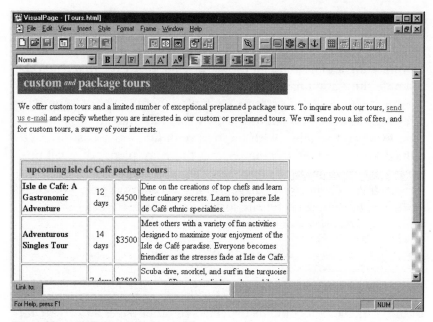

VisualPage Web page design tool

There are many applications that help you create an HTML file, including programs that will convert formatted documents into HTML codes. These make it very easy to produce a Web page with little effort, but do not always allow you to tailor the page to look just the way you want it to.

It's relatively easy to create an HTML file using your word processor (or text editor such as Windows WordPad); the commands are simple to type in and you do not have to be a programmer to understand the way the codes work. I'll start by giving a very brief overview of how to write your own Web page using a simple text editor - this shows you how simple a language HTML is and how easy it is to publish on the Web!

The main file on any Web site is the first contents page that is usually given the name 'index.html'. To create this file, start your text editor (open the WordPad utility in Windows 95 or the Notepad utility in Windows 3.1x) and type in the following text.

```
<HTML>
<HEAD>
<TITLE>Worldwide Book Sales - contents page</TITLE>
</HEAD>
```

```
<BODY>
<H2>Welcome to the Web site of Worldwide Book
Sales</H2>
We aim to sell more books over the Internet than
any other bookshop. From this Web site you can
see the latest best-sellers and our complete
range of titles stocked.
</BODY>
</HTML>
```

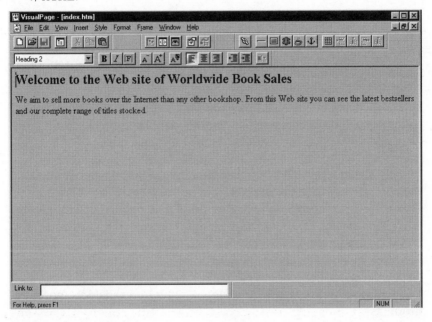

The HTML code above

This is a very basic HTML file that includes some of the HTML codes you will need to use.

1. The first four lines are standard codes that describe the file and the title of this page.

2. The fifth line `<BODY>` defines the start of the main text for the page.

3. The `<H2>` code on the sixth line formats the text as a heading, size two.

4. The eighth, ninth and tenth lines are plain text.

5. The eleventh and twelfth lines are the standard codes to finish off the file.

You might have guessed that these HTML codes work in pairs – <BODY> and </BODY>, <H2> and </H2>: one starts the action, the second stops it. To see how this little Web page would look like if viewed on the Internet, save it as 'index.htm' and start your Web browser software. Select the 'File/Open' file menu option and choose the file you have just created.

Formatting text

Any text that you include in an HTML file will be formatted as plain text – normally a Times Roman typeface in around 9 point (although this depends on the way the user's Web browser has been configured). Reading pages of plain text on a screen is boring, so HTML includes several formatting commands that let you add a little style to your text. The main commands are:

     <B> ... </B>

this will display the text in bold;

     <I> ... </I>

this will display the text in italics;

     <H1> ... </H1>

this will display the text in the largest typesize available – good for headings;

     <H6> ... </H6>

this will display the text in the smallest typesize available – good for notes;

     <CENTER> ... </CENTER>

this will centre any text on the screen (this code might not work on older Web browsers);

     <PRE> ... </PRE>

this changes the font to a Courier fixed-width font.

One of the rather odd points about HTML is that it does not recognize normal line endings. If you enter two lines of text, and press the

'Enter' key a couple of times to separate them with blank lines, a Web browser will join them back together again and display them as one long line. If you want to split up paragraphs or insert a line break in your text, you have to include one of two codes:

```
<BR>
```

this will insert a blank line between two paragraphs of text;

```
<P> ... </P>
```

this defines a paragraph of text and will prevent the next line running on.

To give our Web page a more formatted look, let's add some of these formatting commands to our new Web page for our example company.

```
<HTML>
<HEAD>
<TITLE>Worldwide Book Sales - contents page</TITLE>
</HEAD>
<BODY>
<CENTER>
<H2>Welcome to the Web site of Worldwide Book
Sales</H2>
</CENTER>
We aim to sell more books over the
<B>Internet</B> than any other bookshop.
<BR>
From this Web site you can see the latest
best-sellers and our complete range of titles
stocked.
<BR>
If you would like to send us an order, please
contact us on:
<BR>
<P><I>Telephone: 123-1234</I></P>
<P><I>Fax: 123-1235</I></P>
<CENTER>
<H5>Thank you for visiting our Web site</H5>
</CENTER>
</BODY>
</HTML>
```

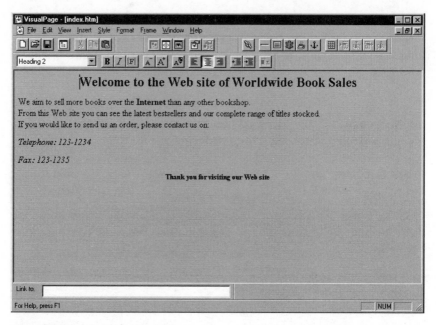

The HTML code on page 145

This sample HTML file provides a basis for any formatting you might want to apply to your text.

Lists and lines

There are special HTML codes that let you create bullet points or numbered lists very quickly. These are useful if you want to put across your main points or the main features of a product:

```
<LI> ... </LI>
```

these codes define the text for a list entry, whichever type of list is being created;

```
<OL> ... </OL>
```

this pair of codes defines the contents of an ordered list which has a number in front of each entry;

```
<UL> ... </UL>
```

this pair of codes defines the contents of an unordered list which has a bullet in front of each entry.

For example, to create a bulleted list of highlights for your product, you would use the following codes.

```
<UL>
<LI>cost-effective</LI>
<LI>easy to use</LI>
<LI>compatible</LI>
</UL>
```

Another example would be to create a numbered list that displays
the steps you need to take when ordering a book.

```
<OL>
<LI>enter the order number</LI>
<LI>enter the delivery address</LI>
<LI>enter your credit card number</LI>
</OL>
```

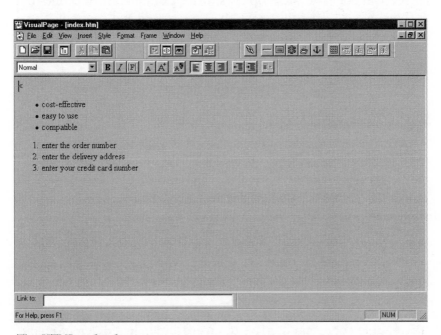

The HTML code above

It's useful to create lines between parts of your text or between
images. There is a simple way to display a horizontal line on the
screen using the <HR> command. This inserts a simple line across the
screen. Some newer browsers (such as Microsoft IE 3 and Netscape
Navigator 2) have enhanced this horizontal line command so that

you can define the width and height of the line;

```
<HR>
```

a simple line across the screen;

```
<HR SIZE=3>
```

an enhanced line which is three pixels high displayed across the screen;

```
<HR WIDTH=50%>
```

an enhanced line which reaches across half the width of the screen;

```
<HR ALIGN=CENTER>
```

an enhanced line which is centred on the screen.

You can combine these options to, for example, create a line that is three pixels high, half the width of the screen and centred:

```
<HR SIZE=3 WIDTH=50 ALIGN=CENTER>
```

Hypertext links

One of the most important features of HTML is that it can include hypertext jumps that link one part of a Web page to another part, one Web page to another page or one Web page to another Web site. All these possible jumps either within a long document or between Web pages use the same basic command:

```
<A HREF>
```

For example, if you want to create a hotword 'order' that will jump to another Web page for ordering products when the user clicks on the word, you would enter the following command:

```
<A HREF='order.htm'>order</A>
```

This simple command displays the word 'order' in a different colour and underlined (to show it's a hotword) and will jump to the Web page 'order.htm' if a user clicks on the hotword.

To create a link to another Web site you would enclose the full URL of the Web site within the quotation marks. For example, if our example Worldwide bookshop wants to include hotword links to publishers on the Internet, it would add the command:

```
<A    HREF='http://www.koganpage.co.uk'>Access
Kogan Page </A>
```

Graphics

Adding graphics to a Web page is normally the next step in Web site production. You might want to include a company logo or a product photograph, or you might want to provide graphical icons that enforce a point. To include an image, you must save the image as a GIF file – most paint programs or image editors will let you save your file in this format. To display an image on a page, use the <IMG> tag. For example, if you have save your logo as LOGO.GIF you would include it on the page using:

```
<IMG ALIGN=CENTER SRC=LOGO.GIF>
```

The extra words in the middle of this command tell the browser to align any text in the centre (vertically) beside the image. If you want to align the image in the centre of your screen, you should use the <CENTER> tag mentioned earlier.

It is good practice to include an ALT description if you display images. This displays a short text description of the image file if the user's browser has been set up not to show images (to save download time). Our image command would now look like:

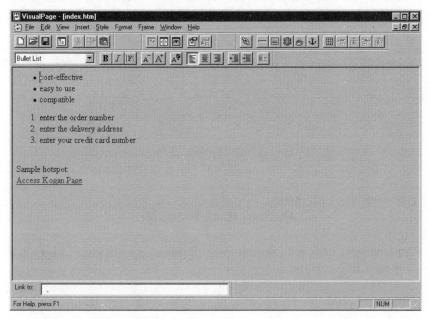

Adding a hypertext link to the page

```
<IMG ALIGN=CENTER ALT="Worldwide Books Logo"
SRC=LOGO.GIF>
```

Finally, you can set up an image as a hotspot. For example, if you want to use a fancy typeface rather than the usual Times Roman displayed on the Web, you could create the text using a paint application, save this as a GIF file and assign a hypertext jump to the image. For example, if you want to assign a jump to the order.htm Web page to an image that has reads 'Order Me' you would enter a combination of the `<A HREF>` and `<IMG>` commands:

```
<A HREF="order.htm"><IMG ALIGN=CENTER
ALT="jump to order form" SRC=ORDER.GIF></A>
```

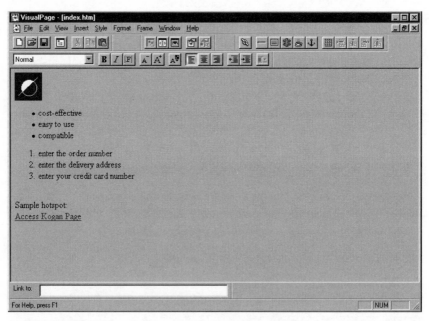

The HTML code above

Putting it all together

We have now covered enough information to create two Web pages – the first is our initial 'index.htm' page and the second is a page that provides information on ordering products, called 'order.htm'. The index.htm page includes formatted text and the company logo together with a jump to link it to the 'order.htm' form.

As an extra feature, I have also changed the background colour of the Web page from the usual gloomy grey to an optimistic white! This was done with an extra word within the <BODY> command that tells the browser to change the background colour to white. The command is:

```
<BODY BGCOLOR=#FFFFFF>.
```

Listing for INDEX.HTM

```
<HTML>
<HEAD>
<TITLE>Worldwide Book Sales - contents
page</TITLE>
</HEAD>
<BODY BGCOLOR=#FFFFFF>
<IMG ALIGN=CENTER ALT='Worldwide Books Logo'
SRC=LOGO.GIF>
<CENTER>
<H2>Welcome to the Web site of Worldwide Book
Sales</H2>
</CENTER>
We aim to sell more books over the
<B>Internet</B> than any other bookshop.
<BR>
From this Web site you can see the latest
best-sellers and our complete range of titles
stocked.
<BR>
We pride ourselves on being:
<UL>
<LI>cost-effective</LI>
<LI>friendly</LI>
<LI>prompt</LI>
</UL>
<BR>
You can contact other publishers on the WWW by
clicking from the list below:
<BR>
<A HREF="http://www.koganpage.co.uk">Access
Kogan Page</A>
```

```
If you would like to buy a book, read our <A
HREF="order.htm">order</A> form.
<BR>
To contact the offices:
<P><I>Telephone: 123-1234</I></P>
<P><I>Fax: 123-1235</I></P>
<BR>
<HR SIZE=3 WIDTH=50 ALIGN=CENTER>
<CENTER>
<H5>Thank you for visiting our Web site</H5>
</CENTER>
</BODY>
</HTML>
```

Listing for ORDER.HTM

```
<HTML>
<HEAD>
<TITLE>Worldwide Book Sales - order
page</TITLE>
</HEAD>
<BODY BGCOLOR=#FFFFFF>
<CENTER>
<H2>Order Information for Worldwide Book
Sales</H2>
</CENTER>
<BR>
It's easy to buy a book from us. Here are the
simple steps to follow:
<BR>
<OL>
<LI>enter the order number</LI>
<LI>enter the delivery address</LI>
<LI>enter your credit card number</LI>
</OL>
<BR>
<CENTER>
Click to <A HREF="index.htm">here</A> return
to our Home page
</CENTER>
</BODY>
</HTML>
```

Multi-column layout and tables

The HTML language is very limiting for designers who want to position elements on a page. Unlike a DTP program that allows you to place text anywhere on the page, HTML tags only allow you to align text to the left margin, right margin or in the centre of the page. Since this leads to rather dull looking page designs, there are several tricks you can use to create pages that have multiple columns. A good example of creating a multi-column Web page is to use a narrow left-hand column to display the contents of the Web site and the wider right-hand column to display the text for the page.

Adding more layout to the page

Multi-column pages can be created using tables. This feature is not available on the older versions of Web browsers, but all the current versions of browsers can display tables.

Simple tables for formatting

Let's start by creating a simple table that formats a table of text with your product names and prices. This is a two column table (name and price) with, say, four rows for four products. In addition, we would like to add a header row that tells the user what's in each column. To create this table, use the following codes:

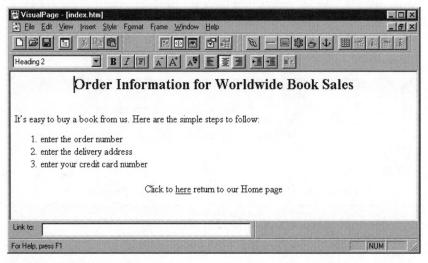

Linking to a second page

```
<TABLE> ... </TABLE>
```

this pair of codes defines the table; you can add the words BORDER=1 to create a table with a border;

```
<TR>
```

this creates a new row in the table;

```
<TD> ... </TD>
```

this creates the entry for a column in the table;

```
<TH> ... </TH>
```

creates a heading row for the table.

Tables have as many rows and columns as you create – if this sounds a little confusing, the code for our example should make this clearer (two columns, four rows, one header row):

```
<TABLE BORDER=1>
<TR>
<TH>Product Name</TH>
<TH>Product Price</TH>
<TR>
<TD>drive belt</TD>
<TD>£15.95</TD>
<TR>
<TD>fan belt</TD>
<TD>£17.95</TD>
<TR>
<TD>drive wheel</TD>
<TD>£22.95</TD>
<TR>
<TD>lock nut</TD>
<TD>£2.95</TD>
</TABLE>
```

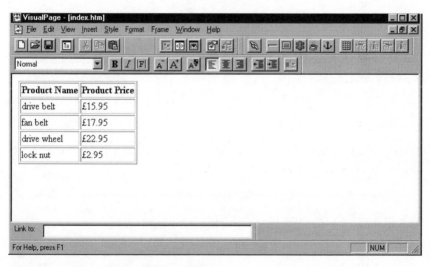

Using a table to display information

Creating an index for your Web page

To use the table command of HTML to create an index panel for your Web page is straightforward, once you understand how the table can be used (see above). When you are designing, it's worth keeping the

BORDER=1 setting on so that you can see how the table appears. Once you are happy with the look of your page, you can switch off the BORDER command.

To create the index page, we will use a two-column table that covers the entire page. There will only be one row within this column. The basic code for our page looks like this:

```
<HTML>
<HEAD>
<TITLE>Worldwide Book Sales - contents page</TITLE>
</HEAD>
<BODY>
<TABLE BORDER=1>
<TR>
<TD>
<B>INDEX</B>
<BR>
Home Page
<BR>
Order Form
<BR>
About the company
<BR>
Product listings
</TD>
<TD>
<H2>Welcome to the Web site of Worldwide Book
Sales</H2>
We aim to sell more books over the Internet
than any other bookshop. From this Web site
you can see the latest best-sellers and our
complete range of titles stocked.
</TD>
</TABLE>
</BODY>
</HTML>
```

You now have a two-column page. In this example, I have just included text in each column, but you could include images or any other HTML command. Typically, the entries in the Index column would be hotwords that link to other Web pages in your site.

Frames

In the previous section I discussed an extension to HTML called
tables. Tables give you more control over the position of text and
graphics on the page. A new feature that is being added to the next
version of HTML is called frames. This lets you set out different areas
of a page that can contain different information. Using frames you
gain far more control over the position of information on the page.
It's possible to create scrolling regions on the Web page and you can
allow the user to change the size of frames to suit his tastes.

Tables provide simple panels

The problem with frames is that not all versions of Web browser will
support frames, so your users will either love your designs or won't
be able to see anything at all. If you do decide to use frames, you
should check that the user's browser is capable of supporting frames.
You can achieve this trick using a CGI program that asks for the version number of the user's browser and displays a frames-enabled Web
page if appropriate. To see how to write a CGI script that can detect
the version number, ask your ISP if they have a library of routines that
can perform this job. If they do not, use a search engine (such as
'www.yahoo.com' to find sites that have CGI scripts.

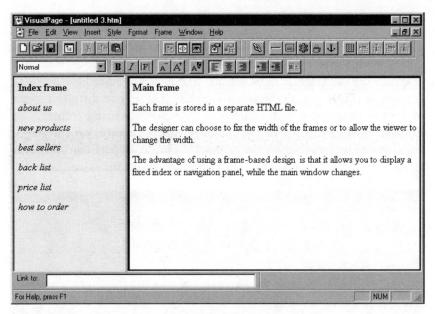

Frames are more complex and sophisticated

Page background

So far, our example Web page has had the default grey background which was changed to a plain white background. It's also possible to change the background to any other colour such as yellow or pink. To set a different background image for a Web page, use the BGCOL-OR word in the <BODY> tag. This lets you define the red, green and blue elements of a colour.

A far more striking look to your Web page can be achieved by using a background image. For example, many sites use a repeating pattern of a company logo as a background. If you create the image of the company logo as a pale grey or pastel shade, text will display on top of it without creating reading problems.

For example, we used our company logo earlier in this chapter as an image displayed on the page. If this logo is repainted in pale grey and saved as a different GIF image file, called BACK.GIF, we can use it as a background (or wallpaper) to the Web page.

The Web browser will automatically repeat the graphic image across and down the page, filling the entire space. This means that if the logo is small, you'll have a lot of images on the repeating pattern.

If it's large, there might be just a few that can fit on the page. To set the background image use the following command:

```
<BODY BACKGROUND='BACK.GIF'>
```

Try and make the background image file as small as possible by using fewer colours – this will make it faster to download.

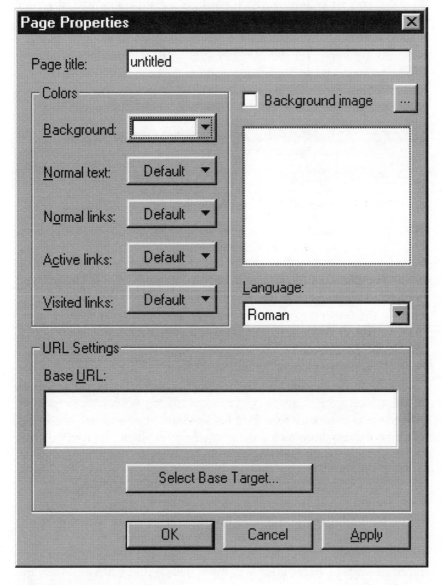

Setting basic page attributes

Adding feedback forms to a Web page

To allow visitors to your site to enter text or choose from lists, you will need to deal with forms. Each Internet company will have a slightly different way of providing this function, so it is best to ask the ISP for a guide to creating forms on your Web page. They will probably send you an example which uses a special program to interpret the text a visitor has entered to either select a page or to send an e-mail message.

Forms are very useful for choosing from fixed options or to allow a user to enter their name and address or comments or catalogue requests. They look a little daunting, but it's worth it to provide a feedback mechanism.

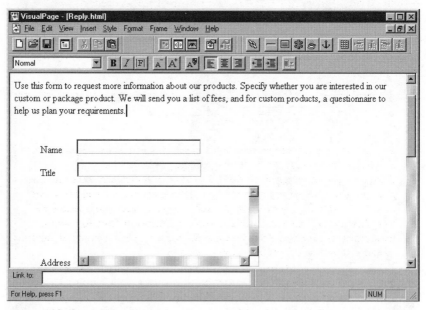

Adding a form for feedback

Design considerations for your Web site

At the start of this chapter, I mentioned the analogy that a Web site will take at least as much time and effort to design as your company's brochure or catalogue. Unfortunately, designing a Web site takes very different skills from traditional graphic design that you would use for your brochure.

There are two main problems when designing a Web site. The first is that you are limited to the HTML series of formatting commands. These let you set size and alignment of text, but you cannot directly position text at a specific point on a page, as you would, say, with a DTP system. The second problem is one of over-design. If you place lots of graphic images in a printed catalogue, it won't cost you any extra. If you place lots of graphic images on a Web page you create a lot of data that takes time to transfer.

A simple Web page that has sparing use of line drawings might take just a couple of seconds to transfer and display on a user's computer. A complex Web page with a small photograph and colourful images might take 40–60 seconds. It is possible for users to prevent graphic images being transferred to speed up access to image-rich Web sites, but this rather defeats the point of good design!

To produce a good Web page, you need to think about how the page will look when viewed using different Web browsers (older versions of browsers cannot display some features) and how long it will take to display.

Tips for page content

1. Do not waste your visitor's download time with gratuitous large graphic images. Use small image files for logos, product photos or icons.
2. Design for the lowest common denominator. Not all Web browsers can display new features, so if you must use new features, try and provide equivalent pages that don't use them. There are still millions of users who access the WWW via a text-based browser and won't see images or fancy formatting.
3. Ensure that it's easy to navigate between the pages on your Web site. Try and include a consistent navigation bar on each page.
4. Tell the user if there is new information available or when the site was last updated. No one wants to read old news.
5. Give the visitor a reason to visit your Web site. Will they be able to provide feedback? Can they download a utility or can you provide them with something no other site can?
6. Provide links to other related sites. This proves you know your visitors will look at other sites and that you're making their Internet visit a little easier.

Browser scripting languages

Up until recently, all the hard work of delivering a Web page to a visitor was carried out by the Web server computer. The user's computer simply asked the server for the page and displayed the results. If you wanted to create animated icon, video or other special effects, these all had to be processed by the remote server computer. It was slow and complex.

Now, the situation has changed dramatically and Web browsers that run on a user's computer have become more intelligent. Web browsers, such as Microsoft's IE or Netscape's Navigator, can run programs on the user's computer. These programs can animate text, create files and carry out other special effects. There are two ways of using this feature: applets and scripts. The two are often confused, but although they can be used for similar jobs, they are different in complexity.

The most common extension is called JavaScript and is the current 'in' way of enhancing the display on a user's Web browser. It's a scripting language that is very comprehensive and is being used by a surprising number of designers – surprising because only the latest versions of Web browsers by Microsoft and Netscape support JavaScript. If you have ever written a macro for your word processor, database or spreadsheet, then you can soon tackle JavaScript. JavaScript was developed by Netscape and, although similar in name, it bears almost no relation to the Java compiled programming language developed by Sun Microsystems (see later for more on Java).

A JavaScript script is a series of commands written as semi-English words within a Web page file (the HTML file that stores the text and formatting commands for a Web page). Think of the JavaScript commands as an extension to the HTML formatting commands. It allows a designer to control the way a Web browser works, but cannot draw graphics or carry out networking functions. (By contrast, the programming language Java can do both the latter but cannot control the functions of a browser.)

Although new, JavaScript has already got a rival in the form of VBScript from Microsoft. VBScript and JavaScript are both text scripts that are embedded within an HTML document. They are usually executed by the client's Web browser, although you can run JavaScript applications on a server. Java and Microsoft's product ActiveX are both compiled languages that can run on the client browser or the server.

To see all the features of JavaScript, you will need to use the Netscape Navigator 3 or Microsoft IE 3 Web browser (Navigator version 2 supported some of the commands). Similarly, to see the features of VBScript, you will need Microsoft IE 3.

Why use a scripting language? Well, if you have created a wonderful site, but want to add an extra pinch of zing, you can use a script to create a moving banner, animate an icon, display dialog boxes on the user's screen to ask questions and much more!

Choosing a scripting language

Although JavaScript has the advantage of a considerable weight of developers using the system and the vast libraries of scripts available to test and tweak, it is more complex to use than VBScript but has the added advantage that it will run (or at least most functions will execute) on both current Netscape and Microsoft browsers. If Microsoft can provide VBScript compatibility for a greater range of browsers then it would be the simplest language for a developer to learn and use.

However, Netscape (developers of JavaScript) will be enhancing JavaScript to work closely with the compiled Java language – and to try and stave off Microsoft's VBScript/ActiveX combination. At the moment, JavaScript has to be the language of choice that allows any developer to create enhanced Web pages with little extra effort.

Applet development

Scripting languages (JavaScript and VBScript) are great ways of adding extra features to your Web page without spending months learning a new language. However, they are simply commands that are interpreted by the user's Web browser.

To create a program that will carry out file processing, complex video or image manipulation or manage other programs, you will need to create an applet. Applets, also called plug-ins, are programs that are downloaded separately from the Web page and run independently on the user's computer. For example, you could create a little applet that will look on the user's hard disk for a copy of Microsoft Word, start Word and open a document file! This would all be invisible to the user and would occur as soon as he views the Web page.

Applets are generally used to allow a Web browser to view video sequences, display multimedia animation or play back live sound. Applets conform to two standards: Java or ActiveX. These two systems are similar but deadly rivals! In each system, the developer designs and develops the program using an object-oriented language similar to C++. This is then compiled into an applet that can be accessed by the Web page designer from the HTML document. The applet and Web page are stored on the Web server and both are downloaded by the client's Web browser. The client computer runs the applet locally.

Since both application development systems require the programmer to learn a new, complex programming language, I will explain the main points of each technology and leave you to download the sample developer kits to try your hand at programming! If you want most of the flexibility but without the programming, you could turn back to one of the scripting extensions that are available for HTML documents.

Active server pages (ASP)

The ASP technology was developed by Microsoft as a way of allowing complex, dynamic pages to be assembled on the server before being sent as a complete page to the client. The system is really a scripting extension to the server (currently supported by several server applications including Microsoft's IIS and O'Reilly's WebSite Pro) that allows the developer to define the content of a Web page as a set of dynamic content elements. These elements might be ActiveX or scripting objects, HTML or data from a database. The ASP server retrieves the latest version of the data, text and objects and combines these together to form the page that is seen by the client. To see ASP in action, visit the Microsoft Web site ('www.microsoft.com') and note the name of the Web documents that you see (such as 'msn.asp') – these are created on the fly by the ASP server.

Cookies

One of the more contentious – and useful – features of the new breed of scripting languages is their support for cookies. A cookie is a file stored on the client's computer that is rather similar to an INI file under Windows. A cookie is officially called a 'persistent client state HTTP cookie' and is defined by the Netscape document 'cookie_spec.html' on their Web site ('www.netscape.com'). A cookie can be written to by a JavaScript script or from Java and allows the Web page developer to save settings on a client's computer. A good example of this would be if you ask a new visitor whether they would like to view the Web site in a particular language. The visitor chooses a language option and this option is saved in the client's cookie.txt file. The next time the visitor visits the site, the Web page checks for this variable setting in the 'cookie.txt' file – if it is present, the script will automatically display the correct language.

There are many different ways of using cookies, but they all stem from the JavaScript command 'document.cookie'. For example, to set up a new cookie entry called 'language' in the 'cookie.txt' file and set this to 'French' you would use the JavaScript command:

```
document.cookie = 'language= French; PATH=/'
```

The last part of this command defines the path for this site so that the cookie entry can be read by any document on this site. To read a value of a cookie entry, you would use a similar command to retrieve the entire cookie string, but then use the substring command to split up the cookie into its components.

Shockwave

An alternative to Java and ActiveX is a programming language called Shockwave. This system, developed by Macromedia ('www.macromedia.com'), lets you add multimedia functions to your Web pages. Using Shockwave you can add animation, presentations, movement and audio using the Shockwave developer's kit.

CGI and Perl scripts

I have left this section to the end, because it's the most complex and best dealt with by a programmer. As you will have seen from the HTML guide, the formatting commands that make up the HTML language are only useful for displaying text and images. You cannot use it to actually do anything. For example, if you want to allow a user to search for text in a database, or display a counter showing the number of users who have visited your site, then you need a more powerful programming language.

The way to add functionality to a Web page is to use something called CGI which lets you run programs from an HTML page. These programs are normally written in a programming language called Perl which is not particularly easy to learn. Normally, the CGI command is entered into your Web page document and this starts a program (or script) written in the Perl language. It's important to check that your ISP can provide this function; even if you cannot use it! If you want to enhance your Web site, it would be worth employing a Perl programmer to create a search program or similar that you could then use.

If you want to carry out any sort of processing on the Web you will need to tackle Perl and CGI scripts. The only way out of this is to set up your own in-house Internet server that provides pre-written solutions and links to a database.

To write Perl scripts you will need to learn the Perl programming language – which is straightforward, but it is probably better to try and get out of this task. There are two options. First look for libraries of pre-written Perl scripts that might already solve your problem. Use one of the search engines, such as 'www.yahoo.com' and look for Perl. The second alternative is to hire a programmer that can manage Perl.

Before you can use any Perl scripts you will need to make sure that you have permission from your ISP. You need to ask for permission to use the '/cgi-bin' directory on their server. Not all ISPs will allow you to write and use Perl scripts on your Web site; those ISPs that cover business customers will normally allow you to use Perl scripts, whereas services geared mainly towards personal users do not allow you to run Perl scripts. Make sure that you check with your ISP that you will be able to run Perl scripts.

What can CGI scripts do?

CGI scripts – normally written in Perl – can enhance your Web site and provide back-room processing power. CGI is not great for adding multimedia extras to your Web site – this is best left to Java or Shockwave – but it can be used for:

● creating a guest book for visitors to sign;

● creating a simple database that visitors can search for information;

● adding a counter to monitor the number of visitors to your site;

● handling forms and interpreting their information;

● running automatic mail programs;

● supporting image maps.

Web page design tools

So far in this chapter I have described the HTML formatting codes that define a Web page. It's not too difficult to enter these codes and create your own page, but it's far easier to get a special software program to help you!

There are now dozens of different tools, called authoring tools, that let you create a Web page without having to enter HTML commands. Some of the tools let you format a document in your word processor and then convert it to a basic HTML file. Other, more advanced tools, let you create your complete Web site and check that the hypertext jumps between pages are working correctly.

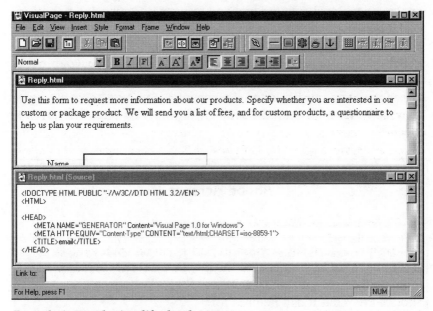

Page design tools simplify development

It is very useful to understand how a Web page is created (as discussed earlier in this chapter), but typing in commands in a text editor takes a long time. It's far easier to drag and drop design elements from a menu and create an entire Web site using templates that reflect your company's image. In short, Web page authoring tools are for those people that want to create a good-looking site without learning a new language.

There are two types of authoring tool. The first provides a nice environment in which to enter HTML codes. The authoring tool will tell you if you have entered a wrong code and will give you a list of codes that you can use. The resulting Web page is often displayed using your normal Web browser. These tools are the older breed of software that helps experienced designers, but does not hide the HTML codes. Programs in this category include HoTMetaL (from 'www.sq.com') and HotDog (from 'www.sausage.com'). There are shareware versions available at these sites that let you test the software before you buy.

The newer, more advanced authoring tools let you create a Web page without having to enter any HTML code. Good examples of this type of software are Microsoft's FrontPage ('www.microsoft.com') and Adobe's PageMill ('www.adobe.com'). Both of these products let you create tables, formatted text and forms without having to type in a single code!

An alternative for anyone that wants a simpler and less expensive system are the add-ons that work with popular word processor packages. For example, Microsoft Word for Windows has an Internet Assistant add-on (available from 'www.microsoft.com') that automatically converts a formatted document into a Web page with HTML codes.

Adobe Acrobat

Adobe's Acrobat software system is an interesting technology that is finding a lot of use on the Internet. It lets you design a complex page using your normal design or DTP software that includes images and text. This is then saved in a special format, called a PDF file. These PDF files are highly compressed and often take up far less space than the equivalent image and text files in a Web page.

The beauty of the Acrobat system is that anyone who has the special viewer software can view your page (or document or book) and the viewer software is available free for almost any computer. Best of all, there is a plug-in accessory that lets most Web browsers view PDF files automatically.

A typical way of using Acrobat would be for a publisher to store sample, highly designed pages of a book as PDF files that are then stored on your Web site. Another example might be a design company showing its design skills. To get a demonstration of Acrobat, visit the Adobe Web site at 'www.adobe.com'.

Storing your Web pages on the Internet

In this chapter you have seen how to design and create your own Web pages, either by typing in HTML commands or by using an authoring tool. Both these systems create your Web site as a collection of files stored on your hard disk. In order to create a Web site that is on the Internet, you need to transfer these files on to your Internet server.

If you are using an ISP for your Web site you will need to transfer your files from your hard disk to your storage area on the ISP's computer. Normally, this is done as follows:

1. Dial into and connect to your ISP as normal.

2. Run your FTP software utility.

3. Use the FTP utility to connect to your storage area at the ISP.

4. Using FTP, transfer your files from your hard disk to the ISP.

5. Leave the FTP program.

6. Start the Telnet utility.

7. Log in to your area on the ISP using Telnet.

8. Move or rename your files (a common change is to change the filenames to '.html').

9. Change the security on the files so that anyone can read them.

10. Log out of Telnet and hang up your modem.

There are plenty of variables that I have not covered in these steps. For example, you will need to ask your ISP for the FTP address and Telnet address you should use to upload your files. Most ISPs will provide you with detailed instructions that show you exactly how to upload your files on their system – once again, most systems vary, so it's worth reading their instructions carefully.

Once you have uploaded your Web page files, anyone can view them by entering your Web page URL into their browser. If you have a domain name for your company, your URL will be similar to 'www.youname.co.uk'.

Companies that have an Internet server in-house need to copy your Web page files to this server. If you have effective security in place on your server, you might still have to use FTP and Telnet to gain access to your own in-house server. Alternatively, if you are using an Internet server program which allows it, you might be able to copy the files over your office network.

11

Setting up your own Internet Server

Why do this?

In the previous chapters you've seen how to market your products on the Internet and how to create effective Web pages. However, the assumption has been that you will be using an ISP (Internet Service Provider) to host your WWW site. This means that you rent a section of their hard disk space on which you can store your Web pages and any other data you want to publish on the Internet. For many businesses testing the Internet waters, this is the cheapest and easiest way of getting a presence. However, if your plans are more ambitious, or if you want to publish a lot of regularly updated information, then you might want to consider setting up your own Internet server.

There are two types of Internet server that you could set up. The first is suitable for small or large businesses and requires a reasonable knowledge of computer setup and maintenance – this is the system I will discuss in more depth over the following pages. The second type of server is far more complex to set up, install and run – you'll need to employ a full-time supervisor to look after it. I'll cover this option at the end of this chapter in less detail: if you plan on setting up a project this complex you either already know how to do it or you should consult specialist agencies.

Your own Internet server

As I have mentioned, most Internet users and small businesses rent resources from an ISP. The ISP maintains the high-speed links to the

Internet, ensures that the hardware and software are running smoothly and provides various other services. You can rent space on their server's hard disk on a monthly basis. For example, you can rent up to 5Mb of hard disk space for around £20–£30 per month. For this monthly fee you will, depending on the ISP, be assured of regular backups and be allowed to write your own simple programs. You will normally also have access to the statistics that tell you who has visited your Web site.

If you want to create a new Web page or if you want to change the information in a data file that users can access, you will have to make the changes on your own computer and use FTP to upload the new files to the server. For businesses that have a lot of data – over 100Mb of data, graphics or text – or companies that want to link a 'live' database or total control over their Web site, then the solution is to set up your own Internet server.

If you set up your own Internet server you will have to provide 24-hour service and ideally you should hire a programmer or system manager to look after it all. This is because you are effectively extending the Internet into your office and your servers will need to keep an accurate address list of every other Internet server.

If this last paragraph has put you off the entire idea, don't worry. The scenario I've described is the difficult way of organizing yourself and I'll cover it in a little more detail at the end of this chapter. For most businesses, the simplest way of installing your own server is to use your ISP to do the difficult work. In effect, you are extending their computer into your office. It works like this.

You will need to install a dedicated computer in your office that runs an Internet server application package. You will also need to configure it and set up your Web pages. This computer is linked to the ISP's main server using a high-speed communications device rather than a standard modem. Typically, you would use ISDN if you have a small Web site or a leased line if you have a bigger and busier site. The main Internet server located at the ISP's office does all the difficult address management and is manned by programmers. Your computer runs your own server application and can accept your own data.

When a visitor to your Web site tries to access one of your WWW pages from their browser, the following scenario takes place. The visitor sends a request to his local ISP with your WWW site as the destination. The server at his ISP looks up your address and contacts your ISP. Your ISP looks up your address and realizes that your Web pages are not stored on its hard disk, so it makes a direct connection to your in-house server. Your server sends the information back to the visitor.

The only difference between this scenario and the usual steps is that your ISP now makes a connection to your computer rather than looking up the data on its own hard disk. In practice, it takes under a second to establish a connection with an ISDN link and just a tenth of a second if you have a leased line in place. To the original visitor, there's no speed difference and he won't realize he has been redirected through an extra step.

Advantages of having your own Internet server

● You can make your Web site as large as you need and store as much data as required, without paying any extra to your ISP for renting disk space.

● You can link your company's database directly to the Web pages so that visitors can access relevant company data – for example, a parts catalogue or directory.

● You can set up secure payment schemes and manage subscriber systems directly and with more control.

● You can supply your Web pages with real-time data, such as changing information on offers, late availability or news.

● You can write sophisticated Web programs that tie in with your company databases, company-wide electronic mail and the Internet.

● You will have full access to the usage reports that tell you who has visited your site, which pages they looked at and which country they originated from.

Disadvantages of having your own Internet server

● It's far more expensive than renting hard disk space on an ISP's server computer.

● It's an extra responsibility for your computer manager or, if you have a small business, for you.

● The running costs are for the link to your ISP are generally around £2,000 per annum for a slow ISDN link and around £6,000 per annum for a leased line.

- You need to buy and set up a new, dedicated computer together with a large hard disk and backup media.

- You need to install and configure Internet server software, which is not always particularly friendly.

What do I need to set up an Internet server?

Creating a presence on the Internet can be a relatively cheap exercise: you need an idea, basic editing skills with an HTML editor, a modem and an account with an ISP. Setting up your own Internet server is a rather bigger job, but it's not out of reach of even small businesses with just a couple of partners – if the business requires it. Here is a basic shopping list for the items that you will need in order to set up and connect your own Internet server.

1. **A dedicated computer that will act as the server**; preferably not your main office network server. There's no point in buying a cheap PC; you'll need a computer that's been designed to run 24 hours a day and has decent cooling, a large hard disk and efficient backup media.

2. **Internet server software**. This manages all the connections to your Web pages and looks after the link to your ISP. There are a lot of different packages available; the most popular is free, but requires a lot of programming and technical knowledge to set up and configure. There is a new breed of server programs that are easy to set up, with the two biggest probably IIS from Microsoft and SuiteSpot from Netscape. Other excellent programs, such as the server package from Luckman, take you through the steps to set up a complex server in easy stages.

3. **Connection hardware to your ISP.** You could just about manage with a high-speed modem to your ISP, but it would only work for small sites that have few visitors. If you do opt for the modem, your ISP's server would automatically dial your number, so you'll need a dedicated telephone line. A small site should have an ISDN link to the ISP. This costs around £200 per year plus call charges, which would probably amount to running costs of £1,500–£2,000 per year. You will need an ISDN adapter (a little more expensive than a good modem). For busy sites, you should invest in a leased

line which is a permanent link between your office and the ISP. This will cost around £6,000 per year but has no call charges – it's permanently open. Check the options that your ISP supports, since they may have restrictions or special deals.

4. **Database tools**. This will let you link an existing company database to the Internet so that any changes made by your operators to the database would be immediately seen by a visitor to your site. The Internet database tools send the query from the visitor to the database and then automatically format the result in HTML codes so that the visitor can view it with his Web browser. If, for example, you are a theatre and want to allow Internet visitors to view availability of seats, you would link your booking database via an Internet query tool so that users could see exactly what is available.

5. **Management tools**. These will let you monitor the Internet server, check to see who is accessing it at any particular time and allow you to analyse the results of usage logs.

6. **Firewall and security products**. These software tools will allow you to connect your Internet server directly to your office network via a high-security product called a firewall. It stops hackers getting into your office network and main office network server. The security products would help to create secure payment or subscriber verification.

Links from your server to the Internet

There are various ways to link your Internet server to the Internet. The one you choose depends on your expected traffic of visitors and the size of your budget. You need to provide a link between your computer and the ISP's main computer (which in turn links to the Internet itself).

Modem

The simplest and slowest method of connecting your server to the ISP is using a modem over a standard telephone line. Very few ISPs support this and it's not worth considering for any complicated application.

ISDN

A relatively cheap and quick solution is to use an ISDN adapter. This is rather like a modem and telephone line: you dial a number and make a connection. The difference is that it's faster to connect (just a couple of tenths of a second) and it's faster to transfer information – between two and four times the speed of a fast modem. An ISDN adapter is a little more expensive than a good modem and you will need to contact your telephone supplier to install a special ISDN line. You will be charged a monthly rental and pay for the amount of time you use the connection.

The way an ISDN link works is simple. When the ISP's computer gets a request from a visitor to visit your Web site, it automatically sends a signal to your ISDN adapter telling it to dial it right back. Your ISDN adapter dials into the ISP's computer and makes the connection. All this takes around half a second and the user won't notice the time lag. Whilst the user is accessing your Web site, you pay a connection charge to the telephone company for the ISDN call you make to the ISP.

Leased line

The third solution for companies that want to link their office networks or have a big Web site is a leased line. This is a permanent connection between your office and the ISP – you pay the telephone company to have a leased line installed, but you do not pay any connection charges for calls. Generally, the leased line will cost around £6,000 per year to run.

In addition to the leased line, you need to connect your Internet server to the leased line which is via a device called a router. These will cost between £1,000 and £3,000 to buy. Lastly, you will need to pay for the service provided by the ISP, which again will cost several thousand pounds (it varies from one to another).

The advantages of a leased line are that it is fast, you have a permanent connection and you know exactly what your costs will be. Although the initial costs are higher than ISDN, there are no call charges to pay for – ISDN costs more for a successful site! Many ISPs that target businesses offer a complete package for a monthly or yearly charge. They will install the router, set up your server and connect you to the Internet. Unless you enjoy this sort of system configuration, it's a good idea to take them up on the offer! However, since charges vary wildly between ISPs, look around before picking your provider.

Statistics from your Internet server

One of the most important tools for monitoring your Web site are the visitor statistics. All servers will generate statistics that list the Internet address of a visitor and the Web pages they have viewed. The problem is normally how to access these log files. If you are running your Web site on a commercial ISP you will normally have the opportunity to access the usage log files for your site – if you pay an extra charge. For example, one of the biggest ISPs in the UK has two types of account. One is cheaper and is aimed at personal users – this does not make usage log files available. The second type of account is far more expensive and is aimed at corporate customers, but does give you access to the visitor log files for your site.

If you are running your own server, you will get immediate access to the visitor statistics, since these will be generated by the server software you are running. The log files record each 'hit' to your Web site. A hit is not the same as a visitor, since a hit occurs each time a visitor looks at a particular page on your site. For example, if a visitor looks at ten pages, your log file would record ten hits – but each hit is generated by one visitor. You can use the log files to see which of your Web pages is most popular – for example, to see how successfully a special offer page is received by your customers.

A log file, whether it's provided by your ISP or by your own server, records a fairly standard set of data for each hit. The log file is saved as a text file that you can read in your word processor with each line of the file representing a different hit.

The start of each line records the address of the visitor – the unique address number that each user is assigned. This might sound ideal – you can see exactly who looks at a particular page at your site and, best of all, you know who they are. Maybe you could even add their address to a database and send them an electronic mail message. This is not the marketing saviour you might imagine. For a start, you cannot send unwanted advertising messages – your Web site could even be shut down if you're considered to be a nuisance. Second, there's a problem with the user addresses that are recorded. Most personal users of the Internet are assigned a different unique

address each time they log on to the Internet, so if you did send an
e-mail, it would probably end up with the wrong recipient.

The one piece of reliable information that you can use from the
user address that's recorded in the log file is the country of origin.
Although each user might be assigned a different address each time
they log on to the Internet, the first part of the address defines the
country in which the ISP operates. You can import the log file into a
spreadsheet or an analysis program and correlate the hits per page
with the visitors' country of origin. In this way, at least, you can see
which are your most popular pages (or products) and in which country there might be a market for the product.

Security for your Internet server

The biggest risk when you set up your own server is that for the first
time any visitor can access files within your company. If you have a
dedicated server that sits in the corner of your office and is not connected to any other computer in the office then a potential villain
could only access the files stored on the server. However, if you connect your own Internet server to your office network – maybe to provide a link to your database or provide electronic mail links – then a
hacker has a way into your office network. This section covers some
of the problems you might encounter when running your own
Internet server – for more detailed information on security, look at
Chapter 9.

When you set up an Internet server you must also take measures
to protect your office computers from outside invasion. Remember,
however, that there is only a real threat if you have your own server
linked directly to other computers in the office.

Most of the security features you will need to implement will be
built into the server software that you use to run the server.
Originally, server software generally provided poor security, since the
Internet was not used for business applications. Now, server software
manufacturers make it very difficult for a hacker to circumvent the
server's normal security features.

The basic concept of security is that a visitor should be able to
view any public Web page or download any public file, but cannot
access any private Web pages or download any private files. This
means that the server software must provide protection against

hackers for FTP transfers and for HTTP requests that are made by a normal Web browser.

As the administrator, you must make sure that the public file areas and the public Web pages are flagged as accessible to any user. It's equally important to protect the other areas – files and folders – that are password protected. Your server software will provide tools that let you set up protected areas.

Firewalls

One of the buzzwords of the Internet is a firewall. It's rather evocative, but in practice it's a rather simple way of creating a block between your Internet server and your office network that will prevent hackers causing havoc. One of the ways in which hackers can get into your server is by sending dummy network data over the Internet that won't be spotted by the server's security systems.

One way of preventing this dummy network data from getting past the server's security is to isolate the way the network data travels through the server. Normally, data would pass into your Internet server from the link to your ISP and then through the Internet server and across to your office network. The firewall sits at this last bridge and verifies every piece of data that comes its way. There are various tricks, such as fitting two network adapter cards into your Internet server which physically separate the Internet server from your office network.

There are many ways of proving security for your network but this book cannot hope to cover them in all in detail. The rule to remember is to make sure you do not neglect this area of your server. It is still very easy for a hacker to gain access to an office network if it is linked to the Internet via a poorly configured server.

Ten steps to setting up your own server

Setting up an in-house Internet server is not a trivial task. Seting up your server and ensuring that it works securely and reliably needs careful planning. The steps you'll need to take when setting up your own server are as follows.

1. Decide if you really need an in-house server. Questions you should consider include – can you provide the support required for a 24-hour operation? Do you need to provide real-time data? Have you a good ISP that can provide help and information?
2. Work out a short-list of ISP providers that offer this type of service. Normally, only the larger or business-specific providers will offer this service. Consider if they provide modem, ISDN or leased line links to your server and the level of the running costs.
3. Try and consider how much traffic you will encounter on your site; this will determine the type of connection to the ISP – modem, ISDN or leased line – that you should configure.
4. If you need to provide links to a database, you might need to employ a pro-grammer to create a suitable application that will take a visitor's search query from a Web page form, use it to retrieve data from a database and return the answer.
5. With your own server you can get more sophisticated in your use of features – you can create complex data applications, provide multimedia and so on. Again, you might need to work with a Web page designer to get the best from your information.
6. Once these elements are in place, you can look at the actual equipment you need. This will include a reliable server computer, a backup device, an unin-terruptible power supply (in case of power cuts), a communications device such as a modem or ISDN adapter and network links to your own office net-work if required.
7. You can now choose your server software. This will probably be tied to a par-ticular type of operating system, for example, Microsoft Windows NT, Novell NetWare or Unix. If you have experience with a particular type of network operating system for your office network then it makes sense to consider the same product as the foundation for your Internet server. The server soft-ware should provide all the tools you require and allow you to provide the services you want.
8. With your ISP account configured and ready, you should now set up your server, the software and check that the data links and Web pages work cor-rectly.
9. Now, finally, you can connect your Internet server to the ISP and test the connections.
10. With all the elements configured it's time to test the online links with the system running. If it all works correctly, advertise and market your Web site to your customers and potential customers.

12

Worked Examples

In this chapter I will discuss some worked examples that show you how different types of companies might set themselves up on the Internet. I have not used real companies, since each company should tailor their presence to their own requirements. Look at these examples and, if you are on the Internet or can gain access to it – perhaps at an Internet café – you should browse the Web sites set up by companies in a similar trade to see how they have tackled the task. Obviously, it's not worth copying another user's site but you might find it interesting to see how the challenges have been tackled. Use these visits to build your own site into a unique and information-rich site.

Self-employed consultant

As a consultant you will want to keep in touch with current customers and with support or professional organizations. You might not find the marketing aspects of a Web page attractive, since you know your target audience and can reach them by personal contact, trade shows or direct mail. However, the Internet would be very useful as a research tool for business consultants and as a support system for computer or IT consultants.

You would probably find the Internet most useful for its electronic mail functions that let you read and send mail to any other customer wherever you are in the world.

Since you might trade under your own name, it's not too important to ensure that you have a domain name registered nor will you particularly want to devote the time and effort to publishing data on to the Internet.

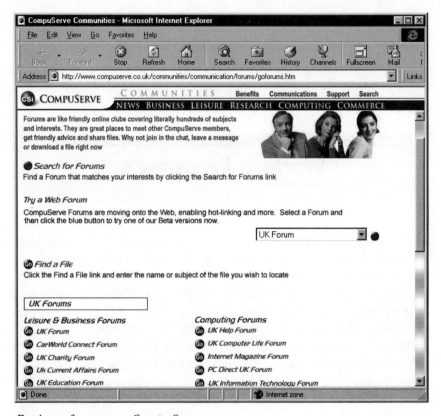

Business forums on CompuServe

Requirements

● worldwide e-mail access;

● using databases for research;

● using support groups to provide feedback to clients;

● possibly a small advertising Web page.

Suggested action

I would suggest that you should look to an OSP that is big enough to provide access telephone numbers with a worldwide coverage. You do not need too many Web publishing options, although a Web browser would be important. Support and discussion groups with other professionals in your field would also help.

Probably the best solution would be to sign up with an OSP such as CompuServe. This company has access telephone numbers across the world – including freephone numbers that are useful if you are dialling from a hotel. It includes up to date online databases of financial data together with hundreds of dedicated support groups for computer and professional activities.

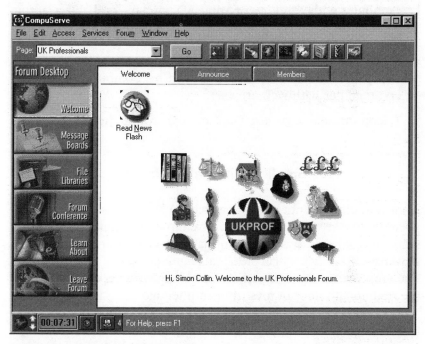

Professional subjects covered

CompuServe assigns you an e-mail address that initially consists of a series of numbers, but you can easily change this number to a friendlier user name, so that your e-mail address would read like: 'SimonCollin@compuserve.com'; in addition, you get a modest Web page area for your own Web site or pages – but without the ability to use your own domain name. The e-mail address is not very friendly (it's a mass of numbers) but you should soon be able to give yourself an easy-to-remember name. With the e-mail system you can send and receive mail messages with any other Internet user. If you want to create a Web page to publicize yourself then CompuServe includes a utility that will do all the hard work for you.

The CompuServe system has a modest monthly fixed fee together with a charge based on the time you spend online. Assuming you will mainly use the e-mail service, this could work out cheaper than another Internet provider with a higher monthly charge. If you find yourself using the online databases too often, you might see your bills increase.

Shopping list

1. Computer with Windows or Apple Macintosh – probably a laptop.

2. Fast modem – if you have a laptop consider a PCMCIA modem that fits inside the laptop.

3. OSP's own dial-up software (provided by CompuServe and others) together with Web browser.

4. Telephone adapter to use your modem around the world.

Small traditional business

A small traditional (not technology-based) business is in an excellent position to use the Internet. For example, a company producing wooden children's toys would normally advertise using colour ads in newspapers and via a mail-order catalogue mailed to a customer list. The emphasis in the company is on quality wooden toys that retain the traditional values of toys from another age.

It is unlikely that too many of your existing customers have e-mail links and again your suppliers (of wood, paint and accessories) might not have e-mail links. Your products are very visual, so perhaps the best use of the Internet would be to publish a Web site with colour photographs of the various toys you produce.

The Internet would be another way of marketing your toys and could lead to export orders from overseas distributors. You might spend your spare time reading the specialist newsgroups for news of how other wood manufacturers cope with a particular paint or finish. You could use the search engines to find distributors with an online Web site and suggest that they carry links back to your Web page.

Customers would not be encouraged to buy sight unseen over the Internet, but they could look at examples and find your nearest distributor. If you had time to travel abroad on business, you would welcome the opportunity but it is unlikely in the near future.

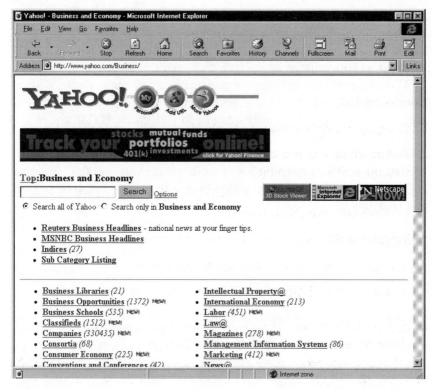

Research online for small businesses

Since you have established a good name for your company and your product range, it would be worth registering your company as a domain name in the countries in which you trade.

Requirements

● Web page with colour photos of product range;

● own domain name with your company name;

● Web page with lists of distributors and price points;

● access to newsgroups and Web search engines;

● minimal e-mail use.

Suggested actions

I would suggest that you set up an account with an ISP that provides a good service to a small company in your country. For example, you could look to Demon Internet that provides 5Mb of free Web space for your Web site. The photographs you include on your Web pages will take up a lot of space (5Mb should be enough for around 20–30 images) so you want as much free Web space as possible.

The ISP can also arrange to register your domain name with a '.co.uk' and a '.com' suffix. You could create a Web page using any of the shareware publishing tools that help you create HTML codes.

The ISP does not provide any of its own content, but you will get access to all the features of the Internet including search engines and newsgroups. If you spend a lot of time online you will find that the ISP's fixed monthly fee with nothing extra to pay except your phone bill reassuring.

Shopping list

1. computer with Windows or Apple Macintosh;

2. fast modem or ISDN router;

3. photo-editing software and HTML authoring software;

4. Internet starter kit (provided by ISP);

5. camera to take photos of products and convert film to a PhotoCD (at most big chemists).

Company supplying academic markets

A company supplying an academic market would be a perfect candidate to use the Internet – nearly every student has an Internet account! This company might sell a wide range of products to schools and universities and want to offer more to visitors to its site. It would want to maintain a good Web site with lots of online data about its products together with extra added-value pages that tell students about other information (perhaps holiday jobs, low-cost travel, course updates and so on).

The company spends a lot of time taking part in online discussion groups to try and keep its name at the forefront with its customers. E-mail is important, but business databases are not so important. There are three people in the company that should have access to the Internet and the office runs on a small network (provided by Windows' built-in functions).

Suggestions

I would suggest that you set up an account with an ISP that supports ISDN links. You would buy an ISDN adapter for your office and connect this to one of the computers and install adapter-sharing software to let each user gain access to the Internet via this one ISDN adapter.

You would have a nice Web page with plenty of information, perhaps just a few images and icons. The main marketing activity would come from your three employees taking part in newsgroup discussions and keeping a close check on e-mails. You could talk to any customer via e-mail – since all your customers have an e-mail link.

The Web site is maintained by you and you would post new information perhaps every few days. You would encourage other users to submit information via your Web form page. The information in your online catalogues would be structured and might have a simple search function written in a Perl CGI script.

Shopping list

1. computers linked in the office via a small network;

2. ISDN adapter connected to one computer;

3. ISDN line installed by your telephone company;

4. adapter sharing software bought from dealer (or supplied with ISDN adapter);

5. Internet software for each user bought;

6. ISP account with 5Mb of Web space and access to visitor logs and CGI scripts;

7. HTML Web page publishing system;

8. Perl script editor.

Medium-sized company publishing on the Internet

A medium-sized company that has a huge list of engineering products together with detailed descriptions and photographs of each. This backlist of data is already stored in a company database and would be useful to publish on to the Internet via your Web site. You would also like to set up a mailing list server that your customers could subscribe to in order to keep them in touch with new products. You would have a second mailing list for your travelling reps who want product updates and marketing information as soon as it's available.

Suggestions

This is a far larger installation and would require an in-house Internet server. The server is linked to the Internet via an account with an ISP using either an ISDN adapter or a leased line. If you think you will use the Internet for more than 3–4 hours per day then a leased line will probably be cheaper.

The Web site would be designed by a specialist company and you would ask the ISP to provide the communications hardware and software to link your company to theirs and on to the Internet. Your employees would enter new details on to the company database which would also be linked to the Web page to allow visitors to search for information.

You would hire a member of the computer department to maintain the Internet server and ensure it's always up and running. The mailing list servers would be part of the Internet server software functionality and would support the two sets of users.

Shopping list

1. good ISP that offers leased line and ISDN connections at a competitive price;

2. ISDN router or leased line adapter supplied by the ISP together with installation;

3. dedicated computer in your company as the Internet server;

4. Internet server software;

5. link to your company database;

6. Web designer to create the software to link your Web pages to the database;

7. computer staff to look after the installation;

8. your own domain name;

9. Web publishing tools;

10. e-mail software for each employee, perhaps with Web browser software for some.

Appendix

Resources of useful Internet sites and telephone numbers for Internet providers.

General search engines

AltaVista
www.altavista.com
Very good directory with entries for most Web sites and FTP stores – a rival to Yahoo!

Ask Jeeves
www.askjeeves.com
An intelligent search assistance that cuts down on the mass of information normally returned by a search engine and, instead, interprets a sentence and returns a few sensible answers.

BigBook
www.bigbook.com
Rather like a business directory, this lets you find a company or product.

BizWeb
www.bizweb.com
A search engine for a collection of business and related Web sites.

Commercial Services on the Net
www.directory.net
Directory of resources on the Web!

Excite!
www.excite.com
A good search engine that provides lateral thinking for searches and finds more related topics than other search engines.

HotBot
www.hotbot.com
This search engine has the largest database of them all and lets you search Web pages and newsgroups at the same time.

InfoSeek
www.infoseek.com
One of the most comprehensive directories of Web pages and resources on the Internet.

Lycos
www.lycos.com
An excellent search engine that provides very good coverage of the Internet.

Magellan
www.mckinley.com
A smaller search engine that has the bonus of a rating and mini-review for each site.

Yahoo!
www.yahoo.com
Provides an excellent listing for most Web sites and FTP stores on the Internet.

Yahoo! UK
www.yahoo.co.uk
A tailored UK version of the well-known search engine.

Yell
www.yell.co.uk
A search directory with a UK bias, provided by the Yellow Pages.

Finding newsgroups

DejaNews
www.dejanews.com
An excellent directory of all the newsgroups that make up Usenet
– lets you search for newsgroups that cover your subject area.

TileNet News
www.tilenet.news.com
Another good search directory that lets you find the newsgroup of
your choice.

Finding people

Four11
www.four11.com
A personal directory of some users on the Internet. Lets you find
the e-mail address of users.

Liszt
www.liszt.com
Directory that covers just about every mailing list, together with a
description and joining details.

WhoWhere
www.whowhere.com
Lets you find a user's e-mail address, telephone number and street
address.

Yahoo!
www.yahoo.com/search/people
A section of Yahoo! that lets you track down the e-mail address of
an Internet user.

Official organizations

British Standards Institution
www.bsi.org.uk
Main site of the BSI. Provides background information on the
organization, together with links to other standards bodies.

Design Council

www.design-council.org.uk

Main site for the influential Design Council organization. Provides links and information on design and product style in the UK.

Marketing resources

Exploit

www.exploit.com

A commercial system that will submit your Web site address and description to hundreds of online search engines for a modest fee.

Internet Link Exchange

www.linkexchange.com

Scheme that lets you exchange your advertising banner with those of other sites.

SubmitIt

www.submitit.com

Similar to Exploit, with more options and different pricing.

WebCounter

www.digits.com

A commercial system of adding a visitor counter to your Web site; it's better to use a CGI script provided by your ISP, but if they don't or won't this site will let you monitor the number of visitors.

Business services online

British Telecom Small Business

www.businessconnections.bt.com

An online magazine for small businesses; updated monthly and contains useful documents, news and articles.

Estates Today

www.estatestoday.co.uk

An online commercial estate agent – useful if you are looking to move offices once your Internet business takes off!

Internet service providers

These provide their own links – the hundreds of other suppliers will use one of these companies.

AOL

0800 279 1234

An OSP that provides an excellent range of its own online databases with Internet support.

BT Internet

0800 800 001

The Internet service arm of the communications giant with full Internet services.

CompuServe

0800 289 378

An OSP that provides an excellent range of its own online databases with Internet support.

Demon Internet Ltd

0181 371 1234

One of the first and the largest independent ISP in the UK. Also provides ISDN and leased lines for company links.

IBM Global Network

0800 973 000

Provides a good service for business customers.

LineOne

0345 777464

Provides Internet access with its own range of database and news services.

MSN (Microsoft Network)

0345 002000

Provides Internet access and a wide range of database, news and discussion group features.

Planet Online

0113 234 5566

An independent ISP that provides Internet accounts and business links.

UUnet Pipex
01223 250 100
Ties with Demon as the major supplier of Internet accounts in the
UK. Also provides ISDN and leased line services.

Turnkey solutions

Apple
www.apple.com
Apple's Macintosh range of servers are available as turnkey
Internet server solutions.

Sun Microsystems
www.sun.com
One of the leading companies in pushing the Internet forward –
developers of Java – and makers of workstations, servers, Internet
software and total solutions.

Creating Web pages with HTML

ActiveX
www.microsoft.com
For all information about the ActiveX programming language that
extends HTML.

Frontpage
www.microsoft.com
An excellent Web management and design tool that's available for
a free trial from Microsoft.

HotDog
www.sausage.com
An excellent product that lets you design Web pages simply – you
can download it for a 30-day trial.

HoTMetaL
www.sq.com
Developers of this HTML authoring system for Windows.

Java

www.java.com / www.sun.com
For all information about the Java programming language that extends HTML.

Shockwave

www.macromedia.com
For information on this multimedia system that extends HTML.

Electronic mail

Microsoft

www.microsoft.com
The general Web site for all Microsoft products and the free Internet Mail program.

Netscape

www.netscape.com
The general Web site for the Netscape range of products and the Communicator suite of browser and e-mail software.

Pegasus

www.pegasus.usa.com
The Web site for the excellent Pegasus e-mail software that is available to download free.

Qualcomm

www.qualcomm.com
Developers of the well-known and excellent Eudora mail software that is in two versions: one can be downloaded without charge.

Internet server software

Apache

www.apache.com
The most popular Web server software on the Internet – runs on Unix and not for a beginner.

Luckman

www.luckman.com

Developers of the very good Web Commander server package that is simple to setup and configure – includes secure credit card transactions and more.

Microsoft

www.microsoft.com

Developers of the IIS server product that ties in with Windows NT operating system.

Netscape

www.netscape.com

Developers of secure standards, browsers and Enterprise Server Web server software.

Novell

www.novell.com

Developers of a Web server product that works with its very popular NetWare range of network operating systems.

O'Reilly

www.ora.com

Publisher of popular Web server software that runs on Windows 95/NT.

Publishing databases on the Internet

Borland

www.borland.com

Developers of a range of database tools, including Delphi and dBASE, that are designed to allow data to be published on the Internet.

Microrim

www.microrim.com

Developers of the R:WEB product that uses its R:BASE database to publish data on the Internet.

Microsoft

www.microsoft.com
Developers of the Access range of database tools that tie in with its Internet server software.

Spider Technology

www.spider.com
Developers of the NetDynamics database product – a powerful solution to publishing data on the Internet.

Business applications

Video Conferencing
CU-SeeMe

www.cu-seeme.com
Software that lets you create a phone or video conferences using the Internet, instead of expensive long-distance calls or satellite links.

Internet Telephone

www.itelco.com
Developers of a software product that lets you use the Internet as a cheap alternative to long-distance telephone calls.

Domain registration

InternetNIC

www.internic.net
The body that registers all domains – if you want to register your domain name or check to see if the name has been taken, visit this site.

News providers

CNN

www.cnn.com
News, headlines, features and weather from around the world displayed on this complex site.

Pointcast

www.pointcast.com

A great idea: uses a screensaver on your computer to display the latest news and financial headlines downloaded from the Pointcast news service.

Software libraries

Cnet

www.cnet.com

A wide range of sites that supply shareware software.

Download library

www.download.com

A collection of freeware and shareware available to download.

Jumbo

www.jumbo.com

A vast collection of best shareware and freeware available to download.

Windows software

www.winsite.com

A collection of Windows software that can be downloaded.

ZD Net software library

www.hotfiles.com

A collection of some of the best shareware and freeware available to download.

Internet Glossary

10Base-T A cabling and connection standard used to carry Ethernet signals. 10BaseT is the offspring of the generic Ethernet specification which defines data transmission of 10Mbits per second using 802.3 data packets over twisted pair cable with telephone-style RJ-45 connectors. Unlike Thin-Wire Ethernet, 10Base-T has a physical star topology that makes it more robust and more secure than its predecessor. However, it needs a central hub. Simple plug-in connectors and 10Base-T's robust and flexible cabling is now finding its way into many more sites than the older co-axial cabling.

Access Provider See **ISP**.

Address book List of names and mail addresses of all registered network users. The Address book is used by the post office to verify that messages are correctly addressed and to deliver them to the correct recipient. The full list of all available users is called the global address book.

Alias Simple name for a user or group of users, interpreted by e-mail software. Using an alias means you don't have to remember complicated mail addresses.

Attachment File linked to an e-mail message and sent at the same time.

Authoring Creating a WWW page using HTML codes to format images and text.

Backbone A very fast communications link that connects major ISPs together across the world. Large companies may also have a high-speed backbone linking many network servers together.

Bit A basic storage unit used in computers; a bit can only be one of two values '1' or '0'. Data is stored in a computer as a combination of bits (eight together are referred to as a byte).

Body Main part of an electronic mail message, as opposed to header and attachment.

bps Bits (binary digits) per second – the measure of data communications speed. It's commonly confused with, but not the same thing as, baud, which refers to the number of transitions made per second and which equals bps only at low speeds such as 300 bps.

Bridge An interconnection device that can connect LANs at the data link level, so allowing similar LANs using different transmission methods, for example Ethernet or Token Ring, to talk. Bridges are able to read and filter the data packets and frames employed by the protocol and use the addresses to decide whether or not to pass a packet.

Browser Software program used to navigate through WWW pages stored on the Internet.

Byte Basic unit for storing data in a computer; a byte is made up of eight separate bits and can store numbers between 0 and 1024. To put it in a more understandable way, a byte is normally used to store a character or digit.

CCITT Comit Consultatif Internationale de Telgraphie et Telphonie: the United Nations group responsible for setting international telecommunications standards. Its recommendations for standard phone lines always start with the letter V (see below).

CGI Common gateway interface: a standard that defines how a WWW page can call special scripts on the Internet server to carry out functions that enhance a Web page; see also **Perl**.

Client Network workstation that communicates with a server; an e-mail letterbox.

Client server A computing system consisting of networked 'clients' which request information and a central 'server' which stores data and manages shared information and resources. Client-server software, or architectures, are trying to reduce the amount of data traffic flowing over the wires between clients and server. It does this by processing data at the server as well as simply retrieving it. For example, a client PC with a simple front-end application asks the server to find all contacts in South London. The server trawls through the database and only returns the correct matches. The alternative is for the client to request the entire database to be sent which it then searches. The difference is subtle, but is the new design on which server-based SQL databases and similar work. The result is that the network is not stressed so heavily. The only caveat is that the server does more by having to run an application in parallel with the NOS.

Dial up A connection that uses a standard telephone line or ISDN link to connect your computer to an ISP.

Distributed processing A technique to enable processors or computers to share tasks amongst themselves most effectively. Each processor completes allocated sub-tasks independently and the results are then recombined.

Domain name The unique name that identifies the location of an Internet server or computer on the Internet. For example, 'microsoft.com' identifies the server provided by Microsoft.

Domain name server (DNS) A computer that stores the names and addresses of every other computer on the Internet. This is used to lookup the correct destination address when you try and access a WWW page or send an electronic mail message. The DNS actually converts the name into a complex and unique pattern of numbers called the IP address.

Duplexing A technique to increase the fault tolerance of networks. In a duplexed disk system, there are two identical controllers and disk drives. Data is written to both via a separate controller. If one goes wrong, the second device is switched in under software control with no effect to the user. This is a more fault-tolerant system than disk mirroring.

E-mail Electronic mail: the biggest use of the Internet is to send electronic mail. You can send messages to any other user on the Internet if you know their address.

FAQ Frequently asked question.

Finger A software program that will go off and retrieve information about a user based on their electronic mail address.

Folder 'Container' for mail messages in a user's mail front-end – rather like a directory under DOS.

FTP File transfer protocol: system used to transfer files between computers linked to the Internet.

Gateway High-level interconnection device which passes packets of data from one type of networking system, computer or application to another by converting the protocols and format of the packets used.

Gateway (e-mail) Interface between different e-mail systems; gateways convert protocols to connect dissimilar networks.

GIF The most common graphics format used to store images displayed on the Internet.

Gopher An (older) menu-based system that lets you navigate the Internet; has now been mostly replaced by the WWW.

Hayes AT The *de facto* standard command set for controlling a modem from a communications program. Even more so than a printer that doesn't work with Epson or Hewlett-Packard software drivers, a modem that doesn't follow one of Hayes' command sets is a software-incompatible oddball.

Header Part of a message that contains the recipient's address, sender's name and any delivery options.

Home page The opening page of a Web site (normally stored in a file called 'index.html').

HTML Hypertext markup language: standard set of codes that describe formatting functions for Web pages including which text is bold, italic, different sizes and how they link to other Web pages.

HTTP Hypertext transfer protocol: the language used by a browser to ask an Internet server for information about a Web page.

Hypertext A way of linking one word or image to another page; when the user selects the word or image, he jumps directly to the new page. This is the basis of navigating around the WWW - if you click on an underlined word in a Web page, it will link you to another section of the page or to another page.

Internet Millions of computers linked together to form a global network allowing users to transfer information between any two computers connected to the Internet. No one person or company controls the Internet.

Intranet Private network of computers within a computer that provide similar functions to the Internet – such as electronic mail, newsgroups and the WWW – but do not have the associated security risks of linking the company to a public network.

IP A unique number that defines a computer that is connected to the Internet. Each time you connect to the Internet you use an IP number that identifies you.

ISDN System that allows digital signals to be transmitted over a special telephone line using a special modem (called an ISDN adapter). ISDN transmits data at 64Kbps – much faster than a normal modem – and makes a call and connects very quickly.

ISP Internet Service Provider: a company that provides one of the permanent links that make up the Internet and sells connections to private users and companies to allow them to access the Internet. If you want to access the Internet you will (in most cases) have to have an account with an ISP. The ISP normally has very fast fixed links to other ISPs on the Internet and provides telephone access numbers for users to dial in with a modem or ISDN adapter.

JPEG File format used to store graphic images (although GIFs are more usual).

Kbps Kilo bits per second: a measure of the amount of data that a device can transfer each second. A fast modem can transfer 28.8Kbps whereas an ISDN adapter can transfer 64Kbps.

LAN Local Area Network: a group of workstations (PCs or Macs) that are physically and electronically linked using cabling. Network software allows each workstation to share files and resources, such as a printer. You can connect your office LAN to the Internet either by adding a gateway to your electronic mail software or by connecting the LAN to an ISP with an ISDN or leased line.

Leased line A permanent communications link between two sites; companies that want to set up their own Internet server in-house would normally choose a leased line between their offices and the ISP. Two ISPs could use a fast leased line to connect to each other to transfer data.

Mail-enabled application A normal application from which it is possible to send mail without specifically calling up your e-mail package. Lotus is mail-enabling new releases of its Windows packages to automatically call up cc:Mail; WinMail supplies macros to mail-enable standard applications.

Mail server A computer that stores incoming mail and sends it to the correct user, and stores outgoing mail and transfers it to the correct destination server on the Internet.

MIME Multipurpose Internet multimedia extensions: a way of sending normal document or data files using electronic mail software. MIME allows a user to send files over the Internet to another user without having to carry out any other actions. Before MIME was developed, you would have to first encode the file and then send it as a text mail message.

Mirroring A means of improving fault tolerance in a network. In a mirrored disk system, two separate hard disks are connected to the same controller. The same data is duplicated on the two drives by one controller. This offers a cheaper, but less secure, fault tolerance than disk duplexing.

MNP A set of error-control standards developed by Microcom Inc. and adopted into the CCITT V.42 standard. MNP allows a modem or communications program to detect transmission errors and request a resend.

Modem A device that lets your computer send and receive information over a normal telephone line. To connect to the Internet you need a modem that will connect to the ISP with which you have an account. A modem works by converting data into sounds that can then be transmitted over the telephone.

Name server A computer that provides a Domain name service. See **DNS**.

Naming services An important development within the last couple of years, spurred on by the importance of WANs. It simply dictates that within a network, each node has a unique address and name of any server or computer can reach and communicate with any other.

NetBIOS Network Basic Input/Output System: a low-level software interface that lets applications talk to network hardware. If a network is NetBIOS-compatible, it will respond in the same way to the set of NetBIOS commands, accessed from DOS by the Int 5Ch interrupt. NetBIOS used to be the de facto standard, thanks to a lack of international standards, but its limitations and age now make it near-redundant.

Netscape Navigator One of the most popular WWW browsers (to download a free trial version, look at 'www.netscape.com').

Newsgroup One area within what's often called Usenet – a newsgroup lets anyone discuss a particular topic. There are over 40,000 different newsgroups that cover just about every subject available. Newsgroups are one of the most active parts of the Internet: you can read messages from other users, comment on them or submit your own message.

Packet The basic unit of data sent over the network during intercommunication. A packet includes the address of the sending and receiving stations, error control information and check procedures, and, finally, the information itself.

PoP Point of presence: a telephone number that links to a modem at an ISP. Normally the ISP will have hundreds of modems linked to local telephone numbers (PoPs) around the country.

POP 3 System used to transfer electronic mail messages between a user's computer and a server (at an ISP).

Post office Central store for the messages for users on a local area network; the post office will also ensure that messages are delivered locally and might have a gateway to route any mail to other post offices or mail systems.

Protocol Rules covering format and timing of messages on a network.

Receive log Tracks total mail received at that point, whether on a mail server or a client.

Remote client User accessing mail without being connected to the mail server's local network. The user can be elsewhere in a WAN, or accessing the mail system via a modem link.

Router A device that lets you connect your office network server or in-house Internet server to the Internet via a leased line. You do not need a router for an ISDN or modem connection.

Rules Method of testing incoming messages for certain conditions (such as the name of the sender or the contents) and acting upon them. For example, a rule could define that any mail from user 'boss' should be moved to the urgent folder.

Shared folder Mail folder accessible to more than one user, functioning as a bulletin board.

SMTP Simple Mail Transfer Protocol: system that allows servers to exchange electronic mail messages in transit from the sender to the recipient.

SSL Secure sockets layer: method of securing a Web site by scrambling the information between the user and server – essential for secure payments and ordering.

TCP/IP Transmission Control Protocol/Internet Protocol: a set of communications protocols developed by the US Department of Defense (DOD), originally for use in military applications. TCP/IP bundles and unbundles sent and received data into packets, manages packet transmission and checks for errors across networks. Originally found binding Unix networks together, its flexibility and portability are making it a de facto standard for any LAN and WAN.

Telnet System that lets you connect to any computer on the Internet (that allows Telnet) and type in commands as if you were sitting in front of the computer. In practice, Telnet is normally used when you are setting up your Web site to create directories, set up security and move files.

UART Universal Asynchronous Receiver/Transmitter: the circuit that converts between the parallel data used by PCs and the serial data used by modems. Serial ports have a UART, while internal modems supply their own. For high DTE rates on systems with a heavy processing load (typically those that use Windows), a 16550A UART provides better, more reliable performance.

URL Uniform resource locator: the full address that defines where a Web page is stored on a server connected to the Internet.

Usenet The most popular collection of newsgroups.

UUencoding Method of converting documents and files to a pseudo-text format that lets them be transmitted as an electronic mail message. This gets around the Internet's inability to transfer mail messages other than text. This has now been largely replaced by MIME.

V.32 The CCITT modulation standard for dial-up modems that allows data-transmission rates as high as 9,600 bps.

V.32bis The CCITT standard for data transmission at 14,400 bps and several slower rates.

V.42 A CCITT standard for error control. It's based on a European error-control standard called LAP M, which also can use MNP Classes 2–4.

V.42bis A CCITT standard for data compression, requiring V.42. Under ideal conditions, V.42bis can provide up to fourfold compression.

WAN Wide area network: multiple small, linked local area networks or a network with multiple servers linked together using public telephone circuits, leased lines or high-speed bridges.

Web browser Software that lets you view Web pages stored on the Internet or on your computer.

Web page Single file stored on a Web server that contains formatted text, graphics and hypertext links to other pages on the Internet. A Web page is created using HTML codes.

Web server Computer that stores the collection of Web pages that make up a Web site.

Web site Collection of Web pages from one person or company that link together with hypertext links to form a home that users can visit on the Internet.

Winsock Utility software that is required to control the modem when connecting to the Internet under MS-DOS or Windows 3. Windows 95 has its own version of this utility built in.

WWW World Wide Web: the collection of the millions of Web sites and Web pages that together form the Web of information that allows a user to see a graphical view of the Internet and the information it contains.

Index